NATIONALISM OR LOCAL CONTROL

Responses to George Woodcock

Nationalism or Local Control

RESPONSES TO GEORGE WOODCOCK

Edited by
Viv Nelles and Abraham Rotstein

new press   TORONTO   1973

ISBN 0-88770-157-4

new press
Order Department
553 Richmond Street West
Toronto 133, Ontario

Manufactured in Canada

Contents

Introduction — *Viv Nelles and Abraham Rotstein*

A Plea for the Anti-nation — **1** *George Woodcock*

Independence: It Won't Be Easy — **13** *Desmond Morton*

The Perils of Patriotism — **21** *Christian Bay*

Separatism for Everybody? — **27** *Norman Ward*

A Conservative Socialism — **31** *George Rawlyk*

Nationalism, Decentralism and the Left — **39** *Bruce Hodgins*

On Independence and Socialism — **47** *Edward Broadbent*

In the Dock of History — **55** *Patrick MacFadden*

The Epitome of a Colony — **61** *D. I. Davies*

The Managed Mosaic — **69** *Donald Smiley*

The Anti-politics of the Anti-nation — **79** *Frank Cassidy*

The Beginning of the Long Dash — **87** *Sam Ajzenstat*

Introduction

To those who are not overjoyed at the electoral prospects offered by our traditional parties, we offer the present symposium ranging into further political horizons. The areas of probing are necessarily circumscribed but the issues chosen – nationalism, local control, and the directions of the left – are of major interest in this country.

Some months ago George Woodcock sent us an article which struck us forcibly with the political dilemma that he posed. Woodcock, a traditional advocate of an anarchist tradition, raised the very topical question of how the newly emerging movements to local control in this country could be reconciled with the equally powerful thrust to develop the national instruments to reinforce our independence from the United States.

We circulated his article to some of the more imaginative political writers in this country and wrote each of them as follows:

Two major political currents are now operating on the Canadian scene: the movement toward greater independence from the United States, and a reawakened thrust for local control – in neighbourhoods (e.g., against expressways), in universities, in industrial plants (workers' control), and among many groups of the poor in our society.

The enclosed article by George Woodcock raises some of these broad questions but concentrates on what he views as an inherent contradiction between the movement to nationalism embodying bureaucratic centralization and the trend to local autonomy.

We are inviting several of the leading political theorists and commentators in this country to respond in their own way to this underlying issue and to any specific aspects of the Woodcock article which they care to take up.

We added that we were interested in having a variety of viewpoints but were mainly covering the broad spectrum of the left.

The present symposium emerged.* It focuses only partly on the theme we had posed; yet it serves at the same time as an opportunity to present the various political credos that are now forming in the writers' minds.

Among these we may note a continuing strong current of suspicion against nationalism (Desmond Morton and D. I. Davies) but a surprising agreement nevertheless that independence in Canada is legitimately in the forefront of our concerns. A traditional plea to abandon nationalism for internationalism (Christian Bay) is followed by strong regional viewpoints: that of the Prairies by Norman Ward and that of the Maritimes by George Rawlyk. Rawlyk and Bruce Hodgins take up as well Gad Horowitz's theme that the bonds in this country between conservatism and socialism act as safeguards for community. Edward Broadbent regards George Woodcock's problem as an opportunity to create a dynamic new order with local autonomy operating as a countervailing balance to the extended role of the state, particularly in the field of industrial democracy or workers' control

Patrick Macfadden shares Woodcock's concern with the growth of the state but finds that a "back-to-the-land" ethic is not a solution. Instead we must confront the large corporation which has co-opted the state as its servant. D. I. Davies probes the continuing colonial roots of Canadian society and calls for a transition from present definitions of nationalism,

*This collection of articles was first published in the April 1972 issue of *The Canadian Forum*. It is now being made available to a wider audience in book form.

largely middle class in character, to new definitions formed by other social classes and ethnic minorities rallying against the present thrust of the state.

Donald Smiley offers a programme of reinforced pluralism which he sees as compatible with Canadian nationalism in a "limited state". He proposes a more independent House of Commons, a dismantling of monolithic structures of provincial education and the protection of small enterprises such as the family farm. A pluralistic community, he feels, offers the real check against the plebiscitary elements of our political system.

Frank Cassidy sees the main danger as the disintegration of the economic institutions of the federal government. He brings an opposite perspective to bear from that of Woodcock, particularly as regards the political heritage of Rousseau. He advocates a centralization of economic power and a decentralization of control of this power to workers, farmers, and students.

Sam Ajzenstat ends the symposium with a cogent political analysis of the conflict of interests and the possibly oppressive nature of Woodcock's small groups. He maintains that if we are to retain our pluralistic way of life within our nationalism we must not decentralize radically.

Woodcock has apparently few enthusiastic adherents among our contributors, but he manages nevertheless to convince us to examine afresh the anarchist postulate of radical decentralization. For those whose eyes have been steadily fixed on the issue of Canadian independence, it is not too soon to ask what forms that independence should take.

We regret the absence of contributions from Quebec. Several invitations to Quebec writers brought, unfortunately, no positive response. What follows, therefore, are some early signals on the evolving political themes in English Canada.

Viv Nelles
Abraham Rotstein

VIII

A Plea for the Anti-nation

GEORGE WOODCOCK

Long ago the pioneer socialist Charles Fourier ("that bizarre genius" as Proudhon called him) posed an ideal transformation of society and of existence. Though he never used the phrase, he foresaw something resembling the Aquarian Age which our contemporary oracles announce as imminent. A time would come, he declared, when all the evil in existence would be purged away, when the salt seas themselves would be transformed into a fluid as delicious and drinkable as lemonade, and beside the lamb would lie down those benevolent creatures, the anti-lion, the anti-tiger, and the anti-wolf.

I do not think many people other than Fourier believed in this Gallic version of The Peaceable Kingdom, but although it is a naive and extraordinary parable, and regarded as a metaphor, it contains the important truth that every evil reveals by implication its opposing good. War makes inevitable the pacifist dream of a world without armies; government ensures the durability of the anarchist dream of a free society ruled by mutual aid; and the evils of the nation-state make inevitable the posing of the vision of the anti-nation as the necessary corrective. It is, I suggest, a vision particularly meaningful to Canadians at a time when, from the Left especially, they are being urged to accept nationalism as a solution.

Indeed, it is one of the paradoxes of the revolutionary tradition that in preaching the universality of man it has encouraged nationalism, and in preaching international liberation it has promoted imperialism. The French Revolution, in which the need to defend the frontiers fanned patriotism into nationalism, and in which the desire to spread the gospel of liberty ended in Napoleonic catastrophe, has been the classic example, followed during almost two centuries with amazing faithfulness. Under the impact of nationalism and imperialism, all the ideals cherished by the precursors of the Revolution vanished; liberty was destroyed by the invention of universal conscription, fraternity by the liquidation of the Girondins, equality by the creation of a new class of *fonctionnaires* from which France suffers to this day. It was a society very different from the small and simple democratic communities of which Jean Jacques Rousseau had once dreamed. It was bred of a collective paranoia, the psychosis that creates aggressiveness out of a sense of persecution; and its almost inevitable result was the transformation of France into a predatory nation, crazed with an incurable undulating sickness named *la gloire*, which recurs at intervals and at present is manifesting itself in a systematic defiance of world public opinion through the continued experimentation with atom bombs in the South Pacific.

It was by inheritance from the French Revolution that one of the persistent elements in the revolutionary tradition of the nineteenth century became an equivocal relationship between nationalism and the movements of the socialist left. In 1848 no cause was more popular among revolutionaries throughout Europe than that of Polish independence, despite the fact that most of the Polish nationalists were aristocratic reactionaries, and when Proudhon called in question, in his classic writings on federalism, this bizarre alliance, he was almost ostracized by the Left of his time. Beneath the resounding ideological battles of the First and Second International, national rivalries played their part, Bakunin's Francophilism competing with Marx's Germanism and neither accepted by British chapel socialism. The fact that these national inclinations were more than skin deep was to be shown not only by the lining up of the mass socialist and labour parties behind their respective militarists in World War I, but also by the way in which, once socialists and communists eventually came to power, they developed into nationalists as extreme as any Tory xenophobe. Lenin, carried through Germany in a sealed train, as if the virus of internationalism he bore would otherwise infect the whole of central Europe, established a regime that under his successors has proved as nationalist as the France of Robespierre, as imperialist as the Britain of Disraeli. Only the anarchists (for Bakunin was an exception in this) and a few socialists on the libertarian Left like Rosa Luxemburg, consistently preserved the internationalism that the whole of the Left at various times has claimed. Now, in 1972, half mankind lives under communist or socialist governments; yet the world republic of the working class, of which we talked so much in the thirties, is still far off when Israelis and Arabs who call themselves socialists hate each other as fervently as Czechs and Russians who call themselves communists.

The cult of the nation has in fact become more, rather than less, widespread than it was in the 1930's, and no less dangerous. With the break-up of the empires, we have more nations than ever, and most of them are militaristic, bureaucratic, undemocratic, xenophobic, and more inclined to spend their resources on war materials and such symbols of national vanity as unnecessary airlines than on developing their countries or raising the living standards of their populations. Today it is not so much the danger of wars of conquest that these proliferating states present, though there is always the chance that some petty dictator's dream of glory may start us down the slide towards global conflict; most of the new nations find blackmail more profitable than war as a means of self-aggrandisement, and the real danger to humanity is that in the crucial quarter of a century that lies ahead of us these intransigent sovereignties will make it difficult to establish any viable worldwide programme for population and pollution control and for the intelligent use of the world's resources.

In saying this, I am admitting that as it has spread from the

highly developed countries of Europe to the less developed
countries of the Third World, nationalism has somewhat changed
its character; its cultural and economic aspects have grown
at the expense of its military aspects, and while technological
change has increased the power of the nation-state to dominate
and restrict the life of individuals, it has also tended to make
nationalism a more democratic phenomenon (in the same per-
verted sense that Nazi Germany was more democratic than the
Kaiser's Germany), since large numbers of the people have,
through the mass media, a sense of being deeply and passionately involved.

Against this background one must view the rise in Canada
of what is rather loosely called nationalism. The reasons for
that rise in Canada are obvious. We have come to the point of
realizing – at least approximately – what, as Canadians, we
are; we have passed the first embryonic stage when the simple
definition of a Canadian was that he was a North American
who didn't happen to be an American. We realize that the anti-
assimilationism of our traditions and the parliamentary forms
we have inherited have made us into a loose association of
regions and peoples of a kind rare in the modern world, where
nationality tends to be associated with ideals of uniformity and
exclusiveness. And we have come to recognize the need for
independence, for liberation from the economic and cultural
pressures that for decades have edged us nearer to the mael-
strom of the American chaos.

I feel an uneasiness amounting to alarm when I observe
nationalism emerging out of this situation. I am told – indeed
I have been told by some of the editors of *The Canadian
Forum* – that nationalism in Canada is not the same as classic
European nationalism, that it is a milder and less dangerous
virus. I am not convinced, though I am ready to make distinctions among those in Canada who call themselves nationalists.

There are some indeed who are Compleat Nationalists, who
see strength coming out of centralization, and who avowedly

wish to achieve the transformation of Canada from a vaguely conceived federation into a nation-state with provincial powers diminished and planning carried out on an all-Canada scale within the framework (despite the startling failure of such measures in another large country, Russia) of massive and centralized nationalization of industry and communications. There are others, equally Compleat Nationalists, whose attitude is luridly characterized by a curious mixture of arid legalism and emotional violence.

But outside the ranking xenophobes and the cold-minded centralizers, there are others who call themselves nationalist, but who really mean that they value the independent, pluralistic, and unpredictable way of existence which Canada offers to the courageous, and who would like to extend and preserve it by freeing themselves from a growing political and cultural subservience to the United States. If these are nationalists at all, they are so in the simplest sense of the word in that they accept the fact that history has made us a distinct people with a common history, inhabiting a clearly defined region. They are not intent on replacing our federal political structure by a national state. They are not exclusive in their loyalties.

Indeed, I would define them as patriots rather than nationalists, bearing in mind the pungent dictum of Orwell, himself a fervent patriot, that nationalism is "power-hunger tempered by self-delusion". And I identify with them, since I have found – to my surprise, after most of my life accepting Dr. Johnson's misleading aphorism – that I also am a patriot in the sense of loving the physical body of Canada and preferring its irregular way of life to that of any other country among the many I have known, with the single and very significant exception of Switzerland, the one European country to reject consistently the path of nationalism. I welcome the great awakening among Canadians to a consciousness that in freeing ourselves from the colonialism of Britain we have become the victims of a much more complex and insidious American colonialism, and I believe that the great task of Canadians in the 1970's is to shake themselves free, even if this means – as it undoubtedly will – a reduction in the standard of living for many people.

But does this mean that we have to add one more to the world's nation-states? It would be tragic to admit it. We are already living, I suggest, at the beginning of what Northrop Frye has called the post-nationalist age (in McLuhan's dim perception, the global village), and we have a start on other countries precisely because we have not gone too far in the direction of the nation-state and because, as I shall show, we already possess in rudimentary form the political organization appropriate to the near future. In that future we have to develop a world community in which sovereignties will be dissolved in those areas where the interests of all humanity are involved – and these I would broadly class as peace, population control, and the safeguarding of resources. At the same time we have to make sure that within these strictly delimited areas of universal interest, every country, every region, every language group, every cultural interest, every locality, and every individual may develop his or its own particular nature and the appropriate institutions, which means a participation in decisions affecting daily existence and lifetime destiny to an extent impossible in most contemporary political systems.

In such a world it is obvious that we must make fundamental adjustments to our political conceptions. Today we conduct political life by means of coercion and confrontation. In a post-national world we shall have to conduct it by co-operation, consensus, and participation, and to devise the means to make this possible involves a profound reconsideration of political structures and political goals alike. There is no point in Canadians becoming late-arriving nationalists in a world where the nation-state, as an effective unit, is already obsolete.

Central to the whole conception of a post-national world is that of federalism, and here Canada has the kind of start that an ill-considered exercise in centralization would merely ruin. Already, in name, Canada is a federation, not a nation, and this fact, which has survived the efforts of centralizers ever since the days of Sir John A. Macdonald, reflects a realization of our country's destiny, to which, almost against their wills, the Fathers of Confederation had to bow. Our geography, dominated by the Shield and the Cordillera, is no more conducive to bureaucratic centralism than the Russian steppes and the wastes of Siberia, while our history (in which unity appears only as a reaction to the American threat) favours the development of a diffuse political pattern, divorced from the imperative of power and made strongly independent by the extension of the federal principle (which is also the participatory principle) to the most basic levels. I believe that Canada, more than any other country in the world today, can develop in a revolutionary way the experiment of Switzerland, which was aborted when the French Revolution diverted attention away from federalism to radical nationalism. We are among the few peoples who still have time to avoid the fever of nationalism and to create the anti-nation: a society open within itself because it is fully participatory, and open towards the world, inclusive and not exclusive; a society which other countries, under the spur of disaster, may find an example worth the imitation.

Merely to sketch such a Canadian society in its entirety would take a book, and one day I may write it, drawing on the neglected federalist tradition, on Kropotkin and Proudhon, on Geddes and Morris, on the Spanish communes and the early kibbutzim, on the Peckham experiment and the direct democracy of Appenzell, on Gandhi's insights into rural reconstruction and Mumford's into the regeneration of cities, and bringing all these untried libertarian visions together in the setting of a country whose physical realities would make it an inevitable failure as a nation-state – Canada.

In concrete terms – and in brief – I propose a hastening of decentralization, a rigorous devolution of power, a universalization of the concept of responsibility. I propose that we abandon the image of the pyramid in thinking of society and substitute that of a mosaic, where the pieces create patterns which are more than themselves, but the patterns remain on the same level as the pieces. In these terms, the Canadian type of federalism, a two-level structure of dominion and provincial governments, with little constitutional link between them, is quite inadequate. This is why all the talk of new constitutions, and of confirming Canadian independence by patriating the B.N.A. Act, is irrelevant. There is a potent relevance, on the other hand, in Proudhon's remark when he cast a solitary vote in France in 1848, "I vote against the constitution because it *is* a constitution." For above all other characteristics, the society of the future must be based on voluntary decisions, and hence it must be liable to perpetual revision.

This means a more varied and flexible kind of social and political organization than we have yet known, an organization whose very suppleness will make it better adapted to deal with the threats of technological change than the present rigid organizations. This makes it difficult to sketch in blueprint detail because it will emerge largely as a reaction against changing technological threats to a rational existence. However, there are certain basic requirements that can be laid down. The starting point of organization would be as far as possible from the national level – in those places where men meet face to face: the shop, the street, the office, the college, the village. This immediately implies the economic consequence of true federalism, which is the control by a community of producers over their means of work, though not ultimately over the destination of the product, for here the locality associations, the groups of residents, embrace the producers in their role as consumers.

Beyond this level one can see certain peculiar Canadian conditions imposing themselves on organization, especially distance and regional differences. At the point where the locality groups, the producers' groups, the factories run by guilds of workers, coalesced into municipalities or rural area associations, there would probably be little difficulty, since these would merely be more participatory forms of existing organizations, concerned largely with municipal affairs and education, though involving themselves in the co-ordination of distribution. But at the point of regional coalescence it is obvious that there would have to be a radical change in the Canadian political structure in the direction of decentralization. The provinces as now constituted are far too unwieldy to be responsive to the day-to-day needs and demands of a socialized community, and their electoral patterns create unnecessary clashes of interest. A small province like Prince Edward Island may be fairly homogeneous, but even in Nova Scotia there are obvious conflicts between the interests of Halifax people and country people, and between those of Cape Breton and the rest of the province. The intolerable situations of Toronto, Montreal, and Vancouver, harnessed to provinces whose governments are dominated by rural and small town interests, is equally obvious, and perhaps the most urgent step of all in making Canadian federalism a reality would be the creation of five free cities (the three I have mentioned plus Ottawa and Winnipeg) of provincial status, and the devolution of the provinces into federations of regions determined by geographical and economic interests. This would encourage the emergence of rural nuclei of activity which would provide a counter-attraction to the cities and perhaps slow the pace of metropolitan growth.

Within this structure, the principle to follow would be the minimization of remote control coupled with the maximization of responsibility through participation. In other words, any decision of any kind that affects only a local group must be reached by that group alone, and by consensus if possible. District and regional boards would consist of elected delegates, subject to immediate recall if they acted against the obvious wishes of their constituents. Beyond that level, provincial and federal assemblies would be elected under similar provisions, which should greatly trim the arrogance of political leaders, and, to ensure the prompt response to rapidly changing social needs that is essential in our era, the referendum and the initiative would be brought into all levels of government.

The great advantage of such a system is that by creating multiple levels of responsibility, all related directly to the basic level through the possibility of popular votes on all important issues, it produces a deeper participation, and while it is impossible to conceive that all conflict of interest will be eliminated, the socialization of the sources of wealth would be likely to reduce them. It will be objected that a federalism which begins by encouraging the most local of interests may disintegrate into parochialism, but my experience is that once people begin to take any interest at all in political or social affairs, their horizons soon spread beyond their narrow personal interests, and since national prejudices can hardly be strong in a country where the central superstructure is minimal and where political mythologies are discouraged, the chances of honest international co-operation based on a sense of world-responsibility are more hopeful among countries than among nation-states.

A more important objection to my suggestions is obviously that based on the certainty of a lowering of material prosperity. It has been one of the unfortunate aspects of the progress syndrome in socialists and communists that they have been unable to conceive a better society except in terms of higher and higher living for more and more people, an eventuality which the steady depletion of the world's resources renders impossible. The anarchists have always been more realistic in this respect. Long before the pundits of the counter-culture, they made a virtue of returning to a simpler existence where work would be done for joy rather than money, and, in that dignified poverty which Proudhon and Paul Goodman extolled, things of the spirit and mind would have more importance than material wealth. Some such consolation we shall all have to accept in any case if we ever embark on the course of making ourselves economically independent of the United States. We shall have to reverse the direction of technology, to use it for the simplification rather than the complication of production, for the reduction in size of manufacturing units and power grids, for the recycling of materials and the use of renewable forms of energy, like sunshine and the tides. (I doubt if we shall have to go back to the horse-plough and the abacus, though that would do us no harm.) All this retrenchment will be easier if we have abandoned the habit of seeing such things, in imitation of the Americans, on a megalomaniac national scale. It will also be easier then to admit that what we have in abundance is land and water, that in a country like Canada the encouragement of the trend towards urbanization has been an aberration, and that industrialization is no solution in rural areas where the need is to bring the lost farmlands back into cultivation and to restore the balance of existence between town and country.

What, after all, are our alternatives at this crossroads of destiny where Canada now stands? With improbable luck, we can allow nationalism to harden our country into a single centralized and authoritarian state that will enter the suicidal competition of the existing nations for space and resources. It is more likely, however, that a policy of nationalism will result not in one, but in two, such states, plagued by the kind of conflict that has wracked the Indian continent for a generation. But a genuine federalism – unlike the disguised statism of Trudeau – would stand a chance of retaining Quebec as an autonomous constituent region, and on Quebec's own terms. Federalism is the one way in which we can turn to advantage the very factors of cultural and geographical diffusion that tell against us as a national state. After all, the Swiss succeeded in keeping themselves together with four languages and cultures; they did so by refusing to accept the temptations of nationalism. But they never became the complete anti-nation. And that leaves it for Canada to create the prototype of the post-nationalist world.

Independence:
It Won't Be Easy

DESMOND MORTON

For the past four years, Canadian independence has been a major theme of discussion in this country. In all their competing varieties, nationalists have found easy access to whatever media of communication Canadians still control. An uncomfortable patriotism has emerged from musty corners in some astonishing places. The contents of attics have been turned into "Canadiana". Ambitious academics have earned promotion and pocket money by scribbling on the topic in the public press. Politicians have assayed the value of nationalism in their party platforms.

The tone, in general, has been shrill, unreflecting, and sometimes irrational. The emotional excitement has almost driven Canadians out of character. One survey, early in 1971, indicated that we were willing to cut our standard of living if that was the price of keeping the true north strong and free. The pollsters must almost have dropped their pencils.

On or about the fifteenth of August, 1971 the mood began to change. Perhaps the dry rot of boredom had already begun to set in even before President Nixon and the United States Congress set out to repatriate two billion dollars' worth of jobs from this country. Certainly, the euphoria faded fast. Outrage survived, exemplified by the Amchitka demonstrations; substance, perhaps represented by the Gray Report, was stuffed back into the filing cabinets. One index of the mood-change was the triumphant re-election of Ontario's Conservative government. Bill Davis's campaign played effectively on the jitters among some of the country's potentially most nationalistic electors. On cue, that erstwhile defender of our independence, Mr. Robert Stanfield, began flailing at Mr. Trudeau, of all people, for queering our neighbourly relations with the United States. At precisely the moment when much that economic nationalists had been saying for years was coming to pass, their fellow Canadians were scuttling for cover.

Once the philosophical and theoretical world of Canadian nationalism catches up with the current turn of events, it will have no difficulty in assigning blame. Scapegoating has been prominent on every nationalist's bill of fare for many years. A sorry lot our balding, overweight businessmen, politicians, and trade union leaders are as they stand in the dock. However, as George Woodcock delicately hints, there is still some room up there for Canadian nationalists themselves. After all, if Canada is still a spindly, weedy-looking plant more than a century after Confederation, some responsibility attaches to those who were in charge of the fertilizer. With nationalists writing much of the country's history these days, the true story of their intellectual ancestors and their collective failure is in some danger of being overlooked.

Take the idealistic young men of Canada First. On the morrow of Confederation, still shuddering at the vulgar commercialism with which the four original provinces had been put together, the Canada Firsters set out to make the new nation worthy of itself. They would fight for a new political morality and for effective independence from both England and the United States. Yet, like their successors, these original Canadian nationalists found great difficulty in fitting their concept of a nation to the untidy complexity of the new Toronto First. If there was to be a real Canadian nation, the young men claimed it had to fit a single model: English-speaking Protestant and Anglo-Saxon.

The test case was Manitoba. Canada First was not responsible for the acquisition of the Red River colony and Rupert's Land: its main purpose was to ensure that the new territory would be an extension of Ontario. By savage exploitation of the murder of Thomas Scott and by intriguing vigorously on the spot, Canada Firsters like Charles Mair, John Schultz, and George T. Denison helped destroy the possibility that Manitoba would develop as a working model of cultural and linguistic duality. The ultimate achievement of Canada First, long after its demise, was the execution of Louis Riel.

A generation later came another school, the imperialist-nationalists, equally determined to free Canada from colonial status. Turn-of-the-century nationalists differed about the means. Could Canada achieve her world role as an equal partner in a powerful imperial federation or should we speak with the voice of a small but sovereign nation? That issue divided the Willisons and the Ewarts, but where they and almost all imperialist-nationalists agreed, was that any world role meant military burdens – troops for South Africa, a Canadian navy, and, by 1916, a promise of half a million men for the slaughterhouse of the Western Front. The efforts paid off. Canada won her seat in the League of Nations and her autonomy through the Statute of Westminster, but she also paid the price of increasing internal division, culminating in the open breach of the conscription crisis of 1917. A majority view of Canadian nationalism conceded hardly an inch to the very different priorities and susceptibilities of French Canada – with utterly destructive political consequences for the whole country.

In short, political nationalism has contributed to some of our most cataclysmic splits. The notion, a little plaintively offered by Woodcock, that our kind of nationalism could somehow be more tolerant and pluralist, finds little historical support. As for economic nationalism, its past proponents have contributed a different but perhaps more persistent form of corrosion.

From the time of the first canal-building, it was apparent that creating the infrastructure for an independent Canada would be expensive. Only time has shown how very unequally the costs would be shared. Among many possible examples, Sir John A. Macdonald's National Policy might illustrate the point. After the Old Chieftain was returned to power in 1878, he proceeded to implement a three-pronged strategy for political and economic independence from the United States. High protective tariffs were imposed, the C.P.R. was built, and, with limited success, the government sought to promote immigration and the settlement of the West. On the basis of these measures, Macdonald has earned recognition by Donald Creighton and others as the leading folk-hero of Canadian nationalism.

Unfortunately, delight and satisfaction with the National Policy declined as one travelled farther from Toronto. The C.P.R., for example, celebrated by song, story, and Pierre Berton, was an extraordinary achievement. It was also enormously expensive and possibly premature. The costs were faithfully borne by generations of Canadians, while the profits, eventually enormous, were carried away by the shareholders, most of them British and American. The national unity forged in a band of steel turned out to be a partnership of exploitation. Prairie farmers found themselves at the mercy of the railway and of the eastern bankers and manufacturers whose interests it served. The farmers' sense of grievance had useful by-products, including a powerful co-operative movement and the C.C.F., but it is hard to claim that the mood of alienation on the Prairies was good for Canada.

To be fair, the railway and the protective tariff gave greater satisfaction in central Canada than in the Maritimes or the West. Ontario workingmen tended to vote Conservative less because Macdonald had helped the infant trade union movement – few of them belonged – than because his policies seemed to be a source of jobs. However, even in the nineteenth century, the ownership and control of those jobs was beginning to slip from Canadian to American hands. Faced by a tariff barrier, U.S. manufacturers simply planted their own branch plants in Canada. They might be small and inefficient, paying low wages and producing high-cost goods, but it hardly mattered. The Macdonald tariff protected native industries and branch plants alike. Indeed, for reasons which were as true then as they are now, the tariff even helped the branch plants to eat up the natives. By 1911, when Laurier and the Liberals offered reciprocity with the United States, their Conservative opponents terrified working-class voters with the claim that free trade would allow the branch plants to disappear south of the border, leaving them jobless.

The point of this recital is not simply to recall that some policies of economic nationalism have proved foolish or unsuccessful: that has been argued repeatedly and with elegance by a succession of Canadian economic historians, including Melville H. Watkins. Instead, it is a reminder that nationalist policies do not automatically deserve support because they claim to aid independence. Like some proposals familiar in our own day, the National Policy perhaps struck its authors as an imaginative, heroic programme for Canadian autonomy. It turned out to be a source of bitter grievance for the outlying provinces and of inefficient, low-wage industries for Ontario. Of course, a shabby record of achievement has never kept nationalism from being the stock-in-trade of politicians bereft of more substantial claims for support. In 1891, Macdonald wrapped himself in the flag to beat Wilfrid Laurier. In 1926, Mackenzie King diverted attention from scandals by a largely spurious attack on Lord Byng. Like some other Quebec politicians, Maurice Duplessis exploited French-Canadian nationalism throughout his career. The examples could be multiplied indefinitely and even extended to our own time.

Such episodes might be no more than a carping footnote to an eminently forgettable past had Canadian nationalists in the last four years shown much understanding of their own flawed history. On the contrary, Canadian independence has again been appropriated as a largely Ontario and even Toronto-centred concern. Once again, belt-tightening and loin-girding have been urged on behalf of policies which were as obviously self-interested and sectional as any of the past. Even before the blunt intervention of Nixonomics, a suspicion was surfacing in Canada that the current bout of nationalism was chiefly useful in buying votes, selling books, and enhancing careers.

If the crisis facing Canadian independence is half as serious as acres of newsprint and gallons of ink would seem to suggest, four years of non-stop Canadian nationalism have accomplished disappointingly little in either finding realistic policy directions or selling them to ordinary Canadians. It is time to declare a short closed-season on the exploitation of Canadian national feeling. With political promoters of all kinds, from the chambers of commerce to the Waffle all trying to hitch patriotism to their own particular band wagon, no wonder the poor beast looks exhausted. Perhaps we can use the interval to melt down all the worn-out slogans, bring the overused statistics up to date and join with George Woodcock in trying to establish a convincing case for the survival of Canada and an effective strategy for achieving it. It may not be easy.

After more than a century of Confederation, a major question about Canadian independence is still "why?". Not all the reasons are ever allowed to surface, sometimes because they are safer in an inarticulate form. Nothing betrayed the comfortable affluence of many of the leaders of the Committee for an Independent Canada more plainly than their unqualified conviction that Canada must survive. After all, as A. E. Safarian suggests, the direct beneficiaries of most forms of economic nationalism will be the native entrepreneur and the professional. C.I.C. members could hardly admit that for a great many people in Canada, nationalism has regularly served as an alibi for high prices and low wages, and, in some circumstances, for the exclusion of effective trade-union bargaining. To their credit, nationalists of the left have explicitly linked their battles for socialism and independence. Unhappily, their definition of socialism adds up to a mildly repellent nineteenth-century utopia. A comparable vision emerges from George Woodcock's celebration of grassroots democracy and the simple life.

The task of formulating a widely appealing vision of what Canada could be is further complicated by the fact that the struggle to re-establish independence may not be easy or congenial, least of all for libertarian decentralists like Woodcock. It is frankly unconvincing to argue that we can serve the ends of economic independence from the United States by the multiplication of small provinces and the massive decentralization of federal powers. The reverse is true. As Kari Levitt has argued, the prevailing trend to enhanced provincial powers, coinciding with the growing power of the multinational enterprise, has only increased the capacity of corporate executives to extract favourable deals from weak, and even strong, provinces. Bartering federal economic and fiscal powers with the provincial premiers may buy short periods of political peace within Confederation but it undermines the long-range capacity of our constitutional system to serve all of our people and to stand up to outside pressures. As in two world wars, the need for a serious collective effort for national survival will demand greater powers for Ottawa, not less.

The obvious strategic need for centralization will discourage many, like Woodcock, who see an independent Canada as a stage for small, self-governing communities to work out their own terms of existence. The tight self-discipline of a collective struggle will dismay others who conceive of independence as a platform for expressing their distaste for the United States in all its manifestations. Like other countries which preserve an uneasy independence from huge and sensitive neighbours, Canadians will have to imitate the Finns and the Poles by rationing their gestures of meaningless defiance so that we can negotiate effectively when it counts.

We are locked up in North America with a United States which is at last responding to the pressures of its enemies to become more isolationist. That position could be one of hopeless weakness; it could also provide us with the first really convincing and unifying vision of our national purpose that we have ever managed to develop.

Independence: It Won't Be Easy 19

Of all the nations in the world, we are best fitted to learn from the American experience and to show that, on this continent, there is more than one possible model for the good life. It has not been easy to be an American over the past ten years: if all we have learned in watching that experience from the bleachers is an undue sense of moral superiority, we deserve the American fate. Instead, we can still take advantage of our size, our resources, perhaps even our collectivist tradition, to do better. With American experience and the insights Americans themselves are willing to share with us, we can save our cities from the desolation and anarchy which otherwise awaits them. In industry, we can enjoy the freedom to explore the potential of joint public-private ventures and of industrial democracy. In education, we can avoid the preoccupation with technique and mechanistic system. In short, Canadians can begin to use their sovereignty not as a framework for defunct structures, or to safeguard the meretricious, or even as a foundation for utopianism, but as a source of liberation and innovation in the here and now. In one respect, George Woodcock is triumphantly right. Canadian independence is probably only worth having if some part of that independence comes to each of us.

The Perils of Patriotism

CHRISTIAN BAY

As large countries go, Canada is not a bad one. In many respects, I'd say it's by far the best one around in today's unhappy world. But then I think there is something radically wrong with having countries, and especially large countries. Countries like Andorra, Lichtenstein, and San Marino are not much of a menace, either to themselves or to their neighbours. Iceland, too, can pass, and possibly Singapore, although even Singapore is rather too populous to constitute a natural community.

All countries deliberately go about building hothouses for a noxious weed, if we may for a moment compare the human mind and soul to a fertile garden capable of growing beautiful flowers, as well as nourishing vegetables. This noxious weed is nationalism; it is seldom attractive, and is rarely nourishing to the individual mind. Rather, it produces something like an addictive drug: it produces a phony euphoria, creates a dependency, and can lead to lasting disabilities. Worse, perhaps, is the impairment of our political intelligence, notably our ability to be rational about the future and to comprehend the vital, overriding importance of the interests that all of mankind have in common.

Nationalism under any other name, if we may now take leave of the floral metaphor, remains the same phenomenon,

The Perils of Patriotism   21

even when it is patted on the back and called patriotism. In English, as in other languages, the irrational pride that we seek to produce in *our* school children, by way of carefully selected chunks of history and other sleights of hand, is called patriotism, while the indoctrination that goes on in foreign countries we term either nationalism or chauvinism, depending on whether our influential elders like their economic systems or foreign policies.

Countries are not only like social organizations, they *are* social organizations. As all sociologists know, or ought to know, organizations tend to be more autocratically governed the larger they become, and their leaders tend to become more ruthless the more people it seems necessary to push around, or deceive. "Enlightened" executives of giant industrial corporations like to give their employees a *sense* of participating in decision-making processes that affect their own lives, and small armies of social scientists are at their beck and call. "Democratic" governments in wealthy countries have even larger armies of educators and social scientists to draw on, whose accumulated efforts have been so effective that physical force nowadays has to be used against relatively few – mainly against criminals, psychotics, political revolutionaries, and young people with deviant smoking preferences. For the rest, we have become dependably compliant democrats and patriots, properly programmed into believing that our country deserves our supreme loyalty, and that the common people are the real rulers, not the power élite. Actually, there would be no such thing as a power élite in Canada, if we were properly socialized.

I support George Woodcock's plea for an anti-nation in Canada, though he may not agree with all of my argument. I too love Canada's spectacular physical nature, but would not call this patriotism, for I respond with similar emotions to, say, the Alps, or to pictures from the Andes, or the Caucasus, or the rice fields of Indo-China. Moreover, people, and especially children, I find even more beautiful than mountains and meadows, and to me a starving or mutilated child in Asia is no less of a calamity than a battered child in Canada. On this issue, the real one, as distinct from the verbal one, I am sure Mr. Woodcock would agree. Only on one other issue is a disagreement quite clear, and it is hardly a major one: I consider the Swiss as nationalist as the rest of them, and in fact I believe they tend to be more smug than, say, the Swedes or the Austrians. The Swiss rulers are piously conservative, and have grown fat on their traditional willingness to take excellent care, with no questions asked, of the funds of the embezzlers, the gangsters, the dictators, and other crooks from all over the world.

As Philip Slater argues in his superb essay, *The Pursuit of Loneliness* (Boston: Beacon Press, 1970), our individualistic creed and our gadget-oriented economic system have frustrated our yearning for community to such an extent that a radical shift in attitudes, and also in institutions, is bound to come. Man has remained, throughout the ordeal of a capitalist commercialism run wild, a social animal, deeply wishing "to live in trust and fraternal co-operation with one's fellows in a total and visible collective entity".

What man has been given, in Canada as elsewhere in the western world, is a cult of pseudo-community instead. In a word, Canadians are being taught, willingly or not, to take great pride in their country; a we-feeling is being cultivated which, because it is artificial, needs constant reinforcement, and also the props of negative feelings towards outsiders – be they American or Russian or French-Canadian.

Except possibly in times of war, there is in fact precious little of "trust and fraternal co-operation" among Canadians in general, for many reasons, but perhaps chiefly because we have a profit-oriented economic system which is deeply divisive; it alienates one person from another (and from himself, too) and thrives on antagonism between competing or exploiting classes, sexes, ethnic cultures – and, of course, nations. How many jobs would be lost if we stopped producing arms for Washington's counter-insurgency needs?

The nation as a make-believe community has, in the com-

munist as well as the capitalist world, become a major obstacle
to the two kinds of real community that we desperately need,
if the human race is going to hold its own (against the bugs and
other species less ecologically vulnerable than ourselves): the
neighbourhood community and the international community.

The Biblical injunction is to treat every person as thy neigh-
bour. What is valid on this point is that it shows how to con-
nect the two kinds of community, humanity in general and
people that we can and must relate to: we relate fraternally
not by ignoring the interests of those we cannot reach, but by
incorporating a consciousness of solidarity with the human
species when we relate to all those whom we do reach, on our
journeys through youth, adulthood, and old age. It has often
been said that to be a socialist in your own home is more
difficult for the average male than preaching fraternity in
society or the world. Yet the home and the neighbourhood are
where community begins, along with the group with which you
work or study. You either accept a place in the pecking order,
acquire the conventional wisdom, and join the tribal cult of
totems like flags, the cross, the hammer and sickle, the anthems,
royalty, and so on, and strive to reach for the top yourself; or
you try to relate as a human being, and to seek love and mutual
respect and to get by without joining the soul-destroying and
community-destroying competitive games for wealth, power,
and status. You either uphold the false communities of the
nation-states, or you work to build real communities of trust
among individuals and families and colleagues and fellow workers, or among people with the same concerns.

Canada has very much going for it, as nations go. Its nationalism is not yet virulent; its natural resources are enormous; its
inhabitants are by world standards relatively healthy and well-
educated. Yet for all the rhetoric of patriotism, at least one in
every four Canadians lives in deep poverty, while the wealth in
some hands is almost astronomical. Large numbers are unem-
ployed, while others must work for very long hours (and neg-
lect their children) to get by. Many of our old people are dis-

carded like useless tools, left to vegetate in poverty and virtual isolation from the young.

Our leaders make speeches about the need for more jobs and for more international trade, and complain these days that our wealthy neighbours, the Americans, haven't exempted Canada from their measures against other trading partners. If some of Canada's spokesmen privately feel that some Third World countries might need a better trade balance even more than we do, that for some of them the U.S. surcharge may mean thousands starving to death rather than, as in Canada, having to make do without a new coat or a better car, they surely do not express such feelings out loud. The name of the game is the national interest, not human solidarity.

Under the cloak of Canada's patriotism, the real name of the game is private corporate interest, or the use of Canadian minds and bodies and other natural resources for the short-term further enrichment of some of the by-now best-endowed moneyed interests the world has ever seen, particularly in the international corporations.

It is high time we stopped playing these obscene games, while there still are viable natural resources left in this country for our children and grandchildren. The youth of the counter-culture have been the first to say No to these games, and they have had the courage, and sometimes the ability, to build *real* communities of their own. But a much broader based, more political, more knowledge-based, attack on the conventional wisdom is needed.

Our universities must some day soon start leading the way, as the least improbable disinterested champions of the public interest, including our interest in a viable future for ourselves and for the international community. But this means that we must also go to work now to transform our universities so as to rid them of entrenched patterns of servility to vested interests and of their own traditional games of caste and class; and so as to enable them to become real communities of enlightenment, dedicated to continuing experimentation in human relatedness and responsible universal citizenship.

That renowned ex-premier from the far-out West, Mr. W. A. C. Bennett, at one time stated that Quebec in his opinion is a have-not province only with respect to political leadership. I believe his statement applies to all our provinces today, and more so to Canada as a nation.

The kind of national leadership to press for, in my opinion, is one that would expropriate the private expropriators of our natural and industrial wealth; entrust further industrial development to decentralized, public corporations; reduce industrial waste and the production of worthless gadgetry; establish a guaranteed income and divide the work among all those who want to work; and, by way of foreign aid and trade on unfavourable terms, help some of the Third World peoples to develop similarly (I did not say *similar*) viable economic and social institutions.

We cannot afford anarchism in our economically and technologically lop-sided world; we need a strong, responsible government, strong enough to ensure that corporate property rights shall no longer be sacred in this country, and that only the basic human rights shall become inviolate. We do need a government strong enough to do without the mystifying rhetoric of nationalism. Strong enough, too, to allow any province or city or local neighbourhood, or any other part of Canada, the widest possible self-determination, short of only one limitation: the federal economic power to make sure that no part of Canada shall be denied a fair share of Canada's wealth. (I would make an exception for Quebec if Ottawa's rule, even in this kind of Canada, should prove obnoxious enough to lead the separatists to victory and complete political independence.)

In the next century, if there is one, Canadian political leadership must become more enlightened than this, and must incorporate among its urgent concerns a responsibility to guarantee fair shares of its natural and industrial wealth to its Third World trading partners as well – without neglecting, of course, the preservation of the resource base for equally viable lives for our descendants, and theirs.

Separatism for Everybody?

NORMAN WARD

The yearning for a simpler life is a dominant theme in folk-
lore and literature, and the more complex technological society
becomes, the more we are likely to hear of it. Mr. Woodcock,
who speaks of "the American chaos" and the intolerable nature
of our metropolitan centres, is in ancient and honourable company. And I should like to join him: it's one reason why I live,
by choice, on the Prairie.

Paradoxically, the Prairie, with its long history of co-opera-
tives, credit unions, and agricultural and other associations of
all kinds, probably comes as close to Mr. Woodcock's ideally
decentralized society as one could hope to find right now; yet
life on much of the Prairie remains relatively uncomplicated
because of national policies which, despite vast abuse, not only
protect the region from many of the worst threats offered by
the twentieth century, but artificially maintain the income of
its less advantaged parts. Even the despised tariff, the "One
Prairie Province" conference in 1970 was told by T. K. Sho-
yama, gives substantial protection to western industry, and its
removal would actually enlarge the competitive strength of
central Canada.

What I am saying, by way of preface, is that it is not possible
for a national in Saskatchewan, regardless of the sabre-rattling
horrors of nationalism elsewhere, to see in a stronger Canadian

nationhood the ogre observed by Mr. Woodcock. Since the days of Mowat and Mercier, and given all our economic, cultural and even legal development since, wars (not of Canada's seeking) have provided the only chances Ottawa has had to do much more than hold its own in competition with the larger provinces.

This is not to reject Mr. Woodcock's thesis out of hand, or to deny the attraction of its sentimental appeal. He says that he'd like to write a book about a major part of it, which suggests that he has not been able to do justice to himself in three thousand words; and this response to him suffers from a related need to escape into generalization when large and specific argument would be more satisfactory. To avoid mere generalization, indeed, I wish to cite what seem to me to be paradoxes in his case, and to raise a query or two. And to be specific I shall only mention and then set aside a few general propositions raised by matters implicit in his paper.

I do not know to what extent, if at all, European nationalisms offer any guide to an understanding of nationalism in the only bilingual federation located in North America and drawn from sources largely British and French. I do not know if there is any necessary connection between a centralized bureaucracy in such a federation, engaged largely in the peaceful maintenance of minimum national standards, and the kind of nation-state Mr. Woodcock fears. The United States does have a centralized bureaucracy for many purposes, and American national feeling is intense; yet that same feeling exists in a country that is in other ways the most decentralized shambles the world has known.

I do not know, though I doubt, whether the kind of intellectual perceptions of nationalism revealed in this symposium come even close to what nationalism really is, or is all about. Chubby Power, drawing on his experiences as a soldier in the First World War and a minister of defence in the Second, once chided me on a related score with an assurance that the man in the street was real, and took a million forms; and in them all he was the one who pulled the triggers and actually got shot. "But he not only doesn't write books and articles about what he feels", Chubby said, "he doesn't even read them."

I do not know, therefore, whether by taking thought about nations and anti-nations we are likely to have much luck, in the face of the colossally centralizing forces in both public and private technology and administration, in devising local groups that will be autonomous in local affairs. My scepticism is heightened by a number of points made by Mr. Woodcock.

"Any decision of any kind that affects only a local group must be reached by that group alone and by consensus if possible." But who is to decide what affects only a local group? Nothing is more local and elemental than human waste, yet even a small city can create downstream pollution of widespread interest. Rural nuclei, however idealistic, will need machinery, and I am reliably informed that small electrical systems can disturb delicate scientific observations many miles away.

"The referendum and the initiative would be brought into all levels of government." But direct legislation can be as easily totalitarian as democratic, partly because it mistakenly assumes that decision-making consists only of the making: responsibility for carrying out the decision and the choice of those who take the responsibility are omitted from the equation.

"Creating multiple levels of responsibility." But we have had multiple levels of responsibility for decades in all our municipal systems. City councils, parks boards, police commissions, school boards, and library boards no doubt increase participation; they also make it remarkably difficult for a common citizen to find out who is really responsible for what. And they resist virtually all change. Mr. Woodcock rightly points out that at the international level "intransigent sovereignties will make it difficult to establish any viable world-wide programme", etc. Quite so: but one obtuse local operator can be an intransigent sovereignty too; and the more decisions are made locally, the greater the scope he'll have.

With all these and other reservations, I am in fundamental

sympathy with Mr. Woodcock's aims and with what I take to be his main supporting argument. I do not know whether it is possible "to reverse the direction of technology" without authoritarian instruments wholly at variance with his purpose; but it is true that we have barely begun to apply science and technology to whole human beings and to human society as such. I don't know either whether the dangers in trying that may not outweigh the benefits: there is not much so far to lead one to feel optimistic. Mr. Woodcock, whatever one may make of some of his particular observations, is beyond doubt an optimist; and in the 1970's every optimist is precious beyond rubies.

A Conservative Socialism

GEORGE RAWLYK

George Woodcock has perceived a new anti-nation Canada through a perceptual filter largely provided by Charles Fourier. Traditional anarchism has flowed gently into the strange contemporary cult of participatory democracy to produce Woodcock's special brand of federalism where "every region, every language group, every cultural interest, every locality and every individual may develop his or its own particular nature". It is Woodcock's contention that Canada can be radically transformed into the "New Jerusalem" and in the exciting process can provide a noble example for all struggling countries to emulate in the so-called post-nationalist world.

My own particular response to Woodcock's manifesto has been conditioned by my political ideology – a peculiar mixture of Calvinism and socialism – as well as by my continuing professional obsession with tracing the historical roots of Maritime regionalism. It appears obvious to me that in attempting to provide for the regeneration of his native country, Woodcock has presented a somewhat distorted picture of both human nature and of contemporary Canada. One does not have to be a reactionary disciple of Edmund Burke to question seriously the philosophic underpinnings of those increasingly influential proponents of participatory democracy. Recent bitter experience, together with the hard facts of history and social psychology, provide convincing arguments, as far as I am concerned, that most Canadians couldn't care less about actively participating in any kind of governmental decision-making affecting their "daily existence and lifetime destiny". Even in the ideal decentralized political system, a small clique of committed enthusiasts will continue, as they have for centuries, to dominate the decision-making process. Radically restructuring the various levels of government will not radically transform the basic elements of human nature. Apathetic, indifferent, and often ignorant people will in the future set the pace and the tone for an increasingly complex society. In this society, fewer and fewer people, the political manipulators, will be expected to provide most of the answers for the old and new perplexing problems confronting mankind.

In the utopian-liberal-Arminian world, however, in sharp contrast, each man, in theory anyway, possesses sufficient intelligence and concern to participate with his fellows in shaping the essential contours of his existence. Within the framework of this secular religion, progress begets progress and increased wealth produces increased happiness. This fundamental "primitive belief" is something most Canadian socialists and Canadian liberals have in common. In other words, they share what may be referred to as a liberal-Arminian approach to life; members of both groups seem to be content to measure political success in terms of a higher and higher material standard of living for more and more people. And because Canadian liberals and Tories have been more convincing than Canadian socialists in persuading voters that they know how to get to the materialistic Millenium by the shortest and safest route, they have tended to dominate Canadian federal and provincial political life. Is there then to be found in the intense bitterness existing between Canadian liberals and Canadian socialists merely the political confirmation of Freud's observation concerning the "narcissism of small differences"? May it not be argued that many Canadian socialists feel compelled to insist upon the great differences existing between themselves and their political opponents – whether liberal Liberals or liberal Tories – precisely because they subconsciously realize that there is in fact no real distinction?

Not only has Woodcock misread human nature, he has also misread the contemporary collective Canadian mind. And in so doing he has underlined a significant contradiction in his entire argument. On the one hand, he maintains that Canada must be broken down into much smaller, decentralized administrative units. On the other hand, he contends that direct democracy must in a dynamic fashion impinge upon every level of the non-nationalistic "new federalism". But what happens to the Woodcock governmental model when public opinion overwhelmingly endorses the twin evils of greater governmental centralization and, to his way of thinking, the dangerous and backward-looking approach to Canadian nationalism? Surely the recently published Deutsch Report on Maritime Union, for example, provides some proof that many Prince Edward Islanders, New Brunswickers, and Nova Scotians are eager to sacrifice their jealously-guarded provincial rights in order to achieve a new regional identity, an identity based on greater, and not less, centralization. And moreover, at the same time, in a fascinating reversal of roles, Maritimers have become, in addition, perhaps the most ardent advocates of a strong – John A. Macdonald – kind of Canadian federalism. Of course, such was not always the case.

In the immediate post-Confederation period, the three Maritime provinces found themselves on the periphery of the dynamic, westward, transcontinental thrust of the new Canada. Largely bypassed by the flood of immigrants into the interior, lacking the natural and human resources for the new industrialism, the Maritimers sullenly watched their region gradually become a social and economic backwater of despair. Who was to blame? Certainly not the proud Bluenosers! The villain was Ottawa; the damning proof was there for everybody to see. Before Confederation there was, or so the argument went, widespread prosperity, and the entire region shared an unbounded optimism and a feeling of self-importance and pride. It was obviously the "Golden Age of Iron Men and Wooden Ships". But after Confederation, there was merely a prolonged period of economic recession and a growing sense of collective inferiority and bitterness. It is not surprising, therefore, that in the 1870's and 1880's some leading Maritimers advocated secession and the return to a more responsible form of independent local government.

But by the early 1970's, the Maritimers had become virtually dependent upon Ottawa for continued survival. And this dependence has produced a powerful attachment to the strongest possible form of central government. As Premier Campbell of Prince Edward Island recently put it, "Canadian requirements . . . necessitate a strong central government" and for him "Strength . . . means financial strength to provide a sufficiently large economic field within which a central government may exercise political and economic influence towards national ends." And Campbell has been willing to practise what he preaches. In order to achieve short-term economic ends the Premier, supported by the majority of Islanders, has given up control over the economic and social future of the Island to the federal government. They have sacrificed their rich historical traditions as well as their local freedom of action in order to be "Upper Canadianized" – that is, in order to obtain a higher material standard of living. In their explicit anti-antinational response, Islanders, like most Maritimers and possibly most Canadians, reveal the true essence of their political culture.

The Maritime surrender to federal centralization has been, it might be noted, accompanied by an intensifying Canadian national awareness in the region. This new sense of being more Canadian than the Canadians was aptly expressed by a Nova Scotia weekly, the Yarmouth *Light-Herald*: "The soul of our Canada is its freedom of mind and spirit in man. Here alone are the open windows through which pours the sunlight of

human spirit. Here alone is human dignity not a dream. But
AN ACCOMPLISHMENT."

Maritimers – as Premier Campbell put it – now "Canadians
before we're anything else" – obviously want simpler, stronger,
and fewer governmental structures to worry about. They do
not want to have constructed artificial barriers which might
hinder the flow of aid from Ottawa to themselves. They remain
obsessed with practical "bread and butter issues" – that is what
government and politics are all about! The editor of the Char-
lottetown *Guardian* succinctly expressed this view when he
observed in May 1967, "Constitutions butter few parsnips."
Another Maritime newspaper made exactly the same point in
Expo year: "Politicians and intellectuals are so busy arguing
about decorating the Christmas tree that there is nobody out
in the kitchen to get the dinner on." As long as somebody,
somewhere, is preparing the dinner, most Maritimers will be
content if, while picking their teeth, they can continue criticizing
the Upper Canadian cooks.

As far as some observers are concerned, Maritimers have
little choice but to do what their federal overlords want them
to do. For their growing dependency has encouraged the growth
of what may be regarded as a Maritime colonial mentality. In
his brilliant study, *The Colonizer and the Colonized*, Albert
Memmi suggests that the colonized eventually come, uncon-
sciously, to believe and to act according to stereotypes of themselves imposed by their colonial masters. This is precisely what
a disconcerting number of Maritimers have done.

Canada, as an anti-nation, with a revolutionary new complex
of governmental structures giving renewed sense of purpose to
North American existence, is an impossible dream. But a conservative socialism, appealing as much to the heart as to the
head, may not be. Canadian socialism – as concerned with
conserving as with changing aspects of society – seems to provide the political means by which a separate and distinct
Canada can continue to exist. It was said that John A. Mac-

donald was a successful politician because he "had a hold not only upon the popular intellect and imagination, but upon the popular heart". What Canadian socialism has largely failed to do is to appeal to the "popular heart". Any successful Canadian political party must be able to tap the reservoirs of "fear" and "pride" which are to be found running deep beneath the surface of the collective Canadian psyche. Carefully conceived and brilliantly researched party platforms, unless they take into explicit account their social psychological dimension, are bound to be callously disregarded by most Canadians.

Over and over again the C.C.F. and N.D.P. have failed to neutralize the deep-rooted popular fear concerning the radical societal changes they advocated. Too often the heady rhetoric of change for the sake of change and vitriolic anti-establishment abuse have alienated the already confused and disoriented voter. It is interesting to note that when Canadian socialists do convincingly show that they have as much concern about conserving worth-while societal values threatened by change as they have with actually implementing change, they invariably succeed. The last Saskatchewan and Manitoban provincial election campaigns immediately come to mind. The lesson to be learned by the N.D.P. is an obvious one – there must be a viable and clearly articulated *conservative* thrust in Canadian socialism; the N.D.P., in other words, must be just as concerned with conserving as it is with transforming certain aspects of Canadian life.

There is also "pride" to consider – a sense of patriotism rather than a vicious brand of nineteenth-century nationalism. Such a sense of provincial and national patriotism should permeate the conservative socialist ideology of the N.D.P. The shrill rhetoric of the Waffle true-believers is to be carefully avoided. What it proposes to do is to Americanize Canadian socialism – to purify the N.D.P. into a fragmented paranoid politico-religious sect. Not without good reason many Canadian voters, equating the Waffle with the N.D.P., bitterly fear and resent the N.D.P. and all it represents. The only hope for an independent Canada remains a socialist Canada but it is a conservative-socialist Canada. And there may be more than one political route to this goal. For it may be that contemporary Canadian socialism has been so infected by what I earlier called "liberal Arminianism" that it will prove incapable of harnessing the conservative-radical dialectic. If this proves to be the case, another political vehicle will have to be found to save Canada.

Nationalism, Decentralism and the Left

BRUCE HODGINS

In Canada we do not have a choice between the nation and the anti-nation, between nationalism and anti-nationalism. Our choice is between some form of Canadian nationalism, dangerous as that might be, and continued drift towards absorption in American nationalism, seductive and easy as that would be. American nationalism is already too dangerous to Americans, to us, and to mankind.

No reflective person on the Left would deny that nationalism makes it possible for a Love-it-or-Leave-it America both to prolong the fight and drag out the withdrawal in Southeast Asia, as well as to turn against dissent at home and to ignore the war on prejudice and poverty. Nationalism helps make it possible for China to defy every principle of socialism and to back the authoritarian, repressive, right-wing regime in Pakistan. But was nationalism a destructive reactionary force in France from 1941 to 1945, in Czechoslovakia in 1968, in Bangla Desh? Is it a reactionary force in and for Yugoslavia, in Chile? Although the count might be close, more people have probably been killed or betrayed in the name of the love of God than in the name of nationalism. Is God inherently bad? Is sex, technology, progress, drugs, democracy, motherhood (population as pollution)? Was the goodness of the French Revolution all destroyed, as George Woodcock claims, by nationalism, or was it partly destroyed by the greed of man, especially bourgeois men, and by the inherent inconsistencies of extreme rationalism? Many, perhaps even most, as Woodcock claims, of the successor states of the destroyed old formal empires have "militaristic, bureaucratic, undemocratic" regimes which use nationalism to sustain their authority. If so, the example is set by the super-powers, which use nationalism, their own and that of others, to maintain and extend their new and probably more economically exploitive informal empires. But even Woodcock admits that the anti-nation has yet to be created and that Canadian patriotism, like Swiss patriotism, is a good thing. Apparently such "patriotism" is good, while the nationalism of others is bad. Let us not quibble over words. In 1917, both the conscriptionist followers of Sir Sam Hughes and the Francophone followers of Henri Bourassa claimed to be enthusiastic Canadian patriots. So did Diefenbaker and Pearson arguing over the flag (Douglas thought that long debate was silly). Who were patriots? Who nationalists?

In Canada we should and must do without the jingoistic, destructive reactionary aspects of nationalism. We must eschew ranting xenophobia and over-sentimentality; yes, we must eschew "bureaucratic centralism", whether advanced by the misguided of the right, left, or centre. Centralism is not working elsewhere; it is particularly unsuited to the potential greatness of this country. We have twice tried to travel that road before. Centralism (Parizeau take note) is particularly unsuited to the world-wide spirit of our age. It promotes alienation and defeats both political and social democracy. No one on the centre or the Left can support the nationalism of men like John Trent who urge the C.I.C. to lobby the federal government to provide a tax policy conducive to the expansion of Canadian-based multinational corporations bent on exploiting such areas as the Caribbean.

Canadian nationalism must involve a concern and commitment to a potential, possible destiny, as yet unfulfilled. With or without Quebec, it must involve a drive to create in the future, from a vague, confused but nevertheless real conception in the dim and relatively recent past, an open, free, and diverse society separate from the one to the south. It must become a society committed to community, co-operation, social justice and something a little closer to equality of condition than the liberals' equality of opportunity. Given its modest potential power, Canada should attempt, along with other modest countries, to nudge the world for the first time towards international sanity.

Most liberal nationalists (both Conservative and Liberal) do not want to become Americans; they worry about the drift, but they are fuzzy as to what myths and traditions different from those of the United States they wish to preserve and develop. One fears that often they want merely a second America, legally independent but with American consumer and individualistic values, shorn presumably of the United States' racial troubles, its gangsters, and perhaps its reflective radicals and world-wide entanglements. This mindless liberal nationalism would be a half-life, a betrayal of our history. It would signify nothing, nothing but mere survival. Then the critics of nationalism would be correct: nationalism would be an élitist concoction which betrays the people.

Nationalists who are socialists, social democrats, and red Tories must have a nationalism of content. The static and almost bankrupt American Revolutionary tradition is inappropriate for us. Québecois have been having their Quiet Revolution. For English Canadians, their intellectual revolution is yet to come (it may never come and will not come without some degree of nationalism), though its outlines are now becoming clearer.

Our nationalism must strive for a decentralized society, qualitatively and visibly different from and better than the one to the south. This can only emerge from the ideas and traditions of the socialists, the social democrats, and the red Tories. But all of the tendencies of their traditions are not appropriate, particularly their propensity at times to problem-solving through centralism, élitism, and big bureaucracy. Their commitment to diversity and to popular involvement must increase. They must make it very clear, for instance, that multi-culturalism must be more than a liberal commitment to Ukrainian folk dances, that positive discrimination in favour of the Indian is necessary to help him fight assimilation. They must make it perfectly clear that our commitment to the Franco-Ontarian (as well as to the Acadian) is not a last-ditch device to try, through some strange Trudeau-like logic, to keep Quebec in the union. Their encouragement of the Franco-Ontarian must be seen to be secure whether or not Quebec separates. Concerned with community and regional identity (while abolishing regional poverty), they must show greater identification with, concern for, and love of the face of Canada, both its land and water.

They must be somewhat less committed to the traditional operation of the Anglo-Canadian parliamentary system and refrain from seeing the congressional one as the only alternative. One would have thought that Trudeau in Ottawa, Bennett in British Columbia, and now Davis in Ontario, would have shattered their last illusions on that score. Parliament under "majority government" is in danger of sinking to the level of the senate under the Roman emperors. Party discipline and most of the nineteenth-century conventions work against the fulfillment of most of their ambitions, including their nationalist ones. Basing representation solely on the single-member constituency organized theoretically on the Liberal George Brown's "rep by pop" surely must be abandoned. The Establishment's fear of the urban masses has prevented "rep by pop" from ever being fully implemented, and the three- or multi-party system means that there is little relationship between popular will and parliamentary seats. The Parti Québecois was frustrated by the Quebec electoral system. Fifty-seven per cent of voting Ontarians (and probably most of those too alienated to vote) clearly did not want Bill Davis as Premier; yet he has a massive majority in the Legislature, and the public is told that he has swept the province. The slavish dedication to the single-member constituency frequently robs the country and all parties of the public services of some of its best brains, greatest nationalists, and most popular and hard-working politicians, often merely because of the whims of a few hundred voters. Other democratic countries have found ways to lessen these losses. Canadian nationalists must address themselves to these problems.

In recent years many articulate voices have urged us to stop searching for a centralized Canadian identity. Ramsay Cook, Maurice Careless, Ken McNaught, and now George Woodcock have reminded us that our historic identities are fortunately regional and even local. If, however, our Canadian nationalism must involve regionalism and decentralism, we must address ourselves to certain problems which as yet have not been satisfactorily assessed. First, and foremost, how do we fight the multinational corporation and nurture decentralism at the same time, especially when some corporations are becoming more powerful and wealthier than the central state itself? How can Sudbury take on Inco, or New Brunswick even a home-grown (if non-resident) K. C. Irving? Or what does one do with a British Columbia government which loves the multinational giants (except those in liquor and tobacco), cares little for ecology or tomorrow, and wants a customs union with the United States? Somewhere in a new flexible federalism the answers must be found.

Secondly, what about the problem of reactionary localism and municipal politics? It is easy to say, and perhaps true, that these reactionary attitudes are the products of decades of centralist, reactionary conditioning. Toronto authorities, especially those in the area affected, wanted the Spadina Expressway. The Union of Manitoba Municipalities wants to take the vote away from people on welfare and to require persons running for office to own property. We must look to the central N.D.P. government to overrule local reactionaries. In Brandon, the mayor and the local Conservative M.P. demand that the university's Board of Governors uphold Victorian morality and reverse its decision to allow the students to arrange for the sale of prophylactics on campus. In Ontario, as clergymen develop social conscience or social involvement, they find their parishioners turning on them with a venom, or abandoning them for the certitude and individualism of the sects. As educational reformers, many of us would like to see the individual school become more of a participatory community-action centre. Yet after years of centralist and authoritarian indoctrination, the first thing many community school groups would do would be to increase the level of conformism and of externally applied discipline, probably including the return of the strap. All but one of the aldermen of Peterborough voted in favour of allowing snowmobiles on city streets, and several city fathers are openly fearful lest the outbursts of ecology freaks curtail local snowmobile manufacturing. Many local police forces, committed to the age-old concept of punishment and vengeance, with considerable backing oppose penal and bail reform and call for the return of capital punishment. Commitment to consumerism, and problem-solving through the economic-growth ethic, seem stronger at the local level than at any other level.

Thirdly, what about decentralism in the face of the contemporary concentration of both political power and control over the mass media? With millions of dollars, the Ontario Conservative media campaign was centrally run. How can people in a locality possibly contend against misrepresentation, brainwashing, and near slander brought in through the local media by outside direction? The *Telegram* folds; then the all-powerful *Star* fires Ron Haggart, one of our few great journalists, for open partisan involvement, something never forbidden newspaper owners or editorial writers. Robertson Davies, the humane, urbane, and sensitive man of the community, sells his Peterborough *Examiner*, without warning, to what many regard as the worst of the multinational corporations in the media field – one based in Britain, red Tories should note, and one ruled by an ex-Canadian. The paper's quality and role in the community is destroyed; its community-dedicated journalists are alienated and dispersed; its editorial page, now usually written by a bitter, red-baiting, pro-American, Hungarian refugee, displays a social and political line to the right of Réal Caouette and Genghis Khan. Virtually everyone is frustrated. Advertising revenue increases. The people are helpless.

With this concentration of power, conscientious Liberals and Conservatives are pressured into abandoning the best of their traditions. Liberals seem to abandon their opposition to monopoly, privilege, and centralism, their concern for toleration and dissent, for local involvement, equality of opportunity, and the geography of the land. Conservatives seem to abandon their concern for the nation's east-west integrity, its ties to Europe, and its rejection from the beginning of continentalism; they seem to lose their commitment to the nation's social, moral, and political reality standing above the individual economic interests of its prominent citizens, and also their understanding of man's propensity for evil. Conservatives drift towards accepting the worst of liberalism, as Liberals abandon the noble aspects of their heritage. Even New Democrats bleed under pressure from their right wing's commitment to basic problem-solving by economic growth and high wages, and the Waffle, toying with centralism, is itself not unaffected.

Without some form of left-wing nationalism it seems difficult to see how Canada can have a meaningful future. To achieve this, socialists and social democrats who are moderate nationalists need the consolidated help of men like George Woodcock, who will wisely and repeatedly warn us of the dangers of centralism and will want to call what we believe in merely patriotism. We will also need the help of the red Tories.

Red Tories have a highly respectable intellectual position, but as long as they remain Conservatives their politics are hopeless and naive. They only assist and lend some respectability to a semi-monopolistic capitalism which their intellects abhor. They must turn from the pessimism of George Grant, our greatest political thinker, one who makes Marshall McLuhan look like the *avant-garde* bankrupt liberal that he is.

But they must build on Grant's insights. To save their country, they must out-Horowitz Mr. Horowitz and ally themselves institutionally with the Left. W. L. Morton, a few years ago, declared that he was as much opposed to capitalism as he was to socialism. Red Tories must join with the Left to produce a humane and sensitive socialism with which they can live.

The right-wing, American-style conservative, J. W. Daly, recently attacked W. L. Morton for his flirtation with the Left and for having the audacity to suggest that a conservative did not have to rest his faith on a theology of original sin and a belief in the after-life. Red Tories do not want a second America in Canada. If they joined with the Left to help fashion the new society, they could rejoice rather than recoil from Daly's denunciation: "Guileless conservatives should be warned that the Left is not interested in using socialism to preserve Canada. It wants to use Canada to build socialism." Six years ago W. L. Morton stated in *Dimension* that within a decade or so the N.D.P. "will have become the political expression of our economic nationalism". If the young red Tories joined the N.D.P., they would tend to oppose rather than to join its right wing; therefore, any latent continentalism in that party would be further weakened. The move has already begun. As one red Tory student, Harry Underwood, noted recently in Trent University's *Arthur*, the Ontario Conservatives

> are a pale counterfeit of the federal Liberals, pragmatic, comfortable wielding power but not particularly attuned to the needs of anyone. . . . People who believe in conservatism will find they must turn to the N.D.P. instead. . . . Perhaps most important, the N.D.P. is committed to government by participation, widening people's access to provincial departments and giving local communities genuine local government.

On Independence and Socialism

EDWARD BROADBENT

George Woodcock's anarchism leads directly to a profound distaste for all forms of nationalism. He sees nationalism quite accurately for what it has normally been in history: an exclusive, intolerant, xenophobic movement. As a force it has tended to swamp with its negative qualities the positive aspects of both liberalism and socialism with which it has so frequently simultaneously emerged. In Europe, the imperialism and totalitarianism of Napoleon and Stalin, not the democracy of Rousseau nor the libertarianism of Luxemburg, emerged triumphant.

The case certainly can be made that it is either too simple to attribute to "nationalist" forces alone the negative consequences referred to above, or that notwithstanding their more horrific aspects both the French and Russian Revolutions (nationalism included) represented net gains for the majority of those affected. The same could be said of the twentieth-century wars of national liberation in the so-called Third World.

To respond in this way to Woodcock, however, would be to miss what is most valuable. What is required at this time for those on the left in Canadian politics is not a more comprehensive understanding of nationalist movements of the past but an honest warning by someone committed to civilized values about the dangers of nationalism. There are no laws in history. There are only trends and tendencies. And knowledge about the consequences of certain kinds of action can be used to avoid or change what otherwise would have been the case. In short, those of us on the left who want both an independent and socialist Canada should take care to avoid promoting within our country attitudes and institutions which would vitiate our liberation objective. This is Woodcock's positive message.

Like Woodcock I believe it is essential that we regain our freedom from the political, economic, and cultural domination of the United States. I am led to this conclusion as the result of two logically prior judgments or values. The first is that socialism in North America is likely to be achieved much more quickly by Canada's first struggling in that direction. To continentalize our economies and cultures now would be a victory for the right, for such action would only serve to strengthen the already immense power of American-owned multinational corporations on a continental basis and would shatter the existing socialist elements in our agrarian west, our trade unions, and our political parties.

The second reason for favouring independence is that it is almost certainly essential for the preservation and enhancement of French-Canadian society. Although it is possible that an independent Quebec might survive, I think the one-hundred-year-old Canadian argument is still valid: that together our two cultures stand a better chance of survival than does either one on its own.

In general terms my own model of an ideal Canada, say by the turn of the century, is a bi-cultural, decentralized federal society in which working people themselves and their elected representatives would have control and in which the spurious distinction between politics and economics would be irrevocably shattered.

Unlike Woodcock, however, I believe that what we require to achieve a Canada of this kind is a programme or strategy that includes measures to achieve an extension of both state and local control. By stimulating the often latent desire for local autonomy and making it actually real, an important countervailing balance is added to the independence thrust which can only be achieved in Canada by extending the role of the state. The kind of apparent contradiction in this course of action (as seen by an anarchist) is for me no more nor less real than the "contradictions" confronted as a *permanent* aspect of reality by a man who believes in utility and aesthetics, compassion and justice, honesty and consideration, privacy and community.

It must be kept constantly in mind that fundamentally it is neither from the American government nor from the American people that we must regain our independence: it is from American corporations and their misshapen objectives. Similarly, at home it is corporate power that dominates our investment priorities, controls our working people's daily lives, and determines the broad outlines of our cultural and athletic activities. What is needed, simply stated, is to democratize our industrial structure.

Canada is a parliamentary democracy but an industrial autocracy. In a wide range of areas there is democratic control. But in one of the central categories, the economic, autocratic power is assumed to be a "natural" right. At both the national level (national investment and production priorities) and the local level (local control of plant and office) those who make economic decisions which have such a powerful effect on our lives are in most crucial respects responsible to no one but the stockholders. (It is remarkable how these facts as they pertain to the multinational enterprise come like a flash of lightning to Herb Gray in chapter after chapter of the Gray Report.) Indeed, it is assumed that only the most extraordinary "practical" circumstances can justify either government or workers' involvement in economic decision-making.

Both in the development of industrial democracy and in its final realization there will be conflict or tension created by the desire to increase and make more effective local and worker power on the one hand and to extend and make more real the power of the state on the other. It is not the case that either objective is preferable to the other: each is required. Nor is there an absolute principle which can be invoked, either in working towards, or in the final stages of, a socialist economy, to resolve the contesting claims, for example, of higher wages for packing-house workers at a given time and the need to benefit society as a whole by reducing the price of meat to the point where the wage claim would be denied.

Some conflict is inevitable. What is essential for us is to break the present degree of overwhelming private corporate power and redistribute it: some to the workers and some to the state. This redistribution is needed as a means of achieving independence, and beyond that point the division will be required by both federalism and socialism as a permanent aspect of our society. What we want and can expect in the long run is to democratize the conditions for resolving such conflict, not to remove it. In so far as Woodcock seems not to see the need for state power to do this he is wrong. But to make sure that in the long run we do not simply become members of a new super-state we must now complement each collectivist thrust with a counter-improvement in local power. In this, Woodcock is clearly right.

It is not necessary in the pages of this essay to outline the details concerning the magnitude of the problem of foreign ownership of our economy. The story, especially since the publication of the Gray Report, is well known. It is important to note, however, that the Liberal Government's almost certain policy conclusion, the establishment of a screening agency to deal with the future, will be grotesquely inadequate in terms of meeting the needs, precisely because it won't come to grips with corporate power. Such an agency set up by the present government, or by a Tory successor, would fail completely on two relevant tests. First, it would leave unaltered the existing degree of foreign domination of both the manufacturing and resource sectors of the economy. Second, the possibility of such an agency curtailing further growth or expansion of existing foreign-owned firms (as suggested by the Gray Report) has not the slightest chance of implementation by either of our capitalist-oriented parties. I do not make these points dogmatically. The fact is that such action would represent an important ideological shift of the kind not taken by those with power unless under the most extreme pressure. Can any reader seriously imagine either Trudeau or Stanfield even embarking on a plan which would restrict firms' growth in certain sectors (whether foreign or domestically owned) either by prohibiting their access to capital markets or by levying a special tax on them to obtain funds to promote growth in another sector?

What is required is a series of measures, all of which involve breaking into traditional corporate-rights areas at the non-local level:

(1) A whole set of direct and indirect controls exercised by the federal government. These would keep Canadian-generated capital in Canada to be used for investment in areas whose priorities are determined not by the corporations but by our federal and provincial governments. Of particular importance here would be the explicit government direction of Canadian banking and insurance investment-money exclusively into the Canadian economy and exclusively within the Canadian-owned sectors of the economy.

(2) A selective nationalization programme aimed at regaining early control of important resources and manufacturing sectors. A relevant criterion to be met in terms of priority would be the potential for early significant growth on either foreign or domestic markets.

(3) The development and enforcement of an industrial strategy for Canada based on forecast international demand and our own particular advantages in terms of resources and related, domestically controlled, research and development programmes.

These points are, admittedly, simply asserted. However, on

the basis of evidence and arguments brought forward by many others in the past few years, I believe that nothing less than these significant initial incursions into corporate power and influence at the national or federal level will be sufficient to achieve independence. Quite apart from other moral considerations, those who now opt for Canadian freedom must also choose to expand the role of the state significantly. To refuse the latter is to deny the possibility of the former.

As we saw above, it is essential that such action at the federal and provincial level, both for its own sake and as a means of counteracting the inevitably restrictive aspects of a "nationalist" independence movement, be complemented by a simultaneous incursion into corporate power at the level of the work place.

There are many usages of the term "industrial democracy," but for any of them to be appropriate it must include one core characteristic: those affected by a decision must make the decision themselves or have *effective* power over those who do. There is no democracy in a society, with or without a publicly owned economy, whose members have simply the right to advise, to oppose, or to protect.

At the local level it has been Canada's trade unionists who have been primarily responsible for achieving for the average Canadian his present degree of dignity and security. Compared with merely a few decades ago, our organized worker's position is significantly improved. He has paid holidays; his wages are higher and his hours shorter; he can no longer be fired at the whim of an irascible boss. In many respects these same benefits have now also become available to non-unionized workers. There can be no doubt, however, that without the unions these improvements for the organized and unorganized alike would not have materialized. Management's list of "prerogative" powers would have remained as it was at the turn of the century.

What is now required is a qualitative change in the worker's position at work. Means must be discovered for obtaining a direct and effective influence in all those areas hitherto regarded as the absolute prerogatives of management. The guiding principle should be that the more immediate and exclusive an impact a category of activity has, the more autonomous should be the decision-making authority of a given body of workers. For example, job allocation, shift-schedules, product innovation, and discipline should probably be in the exclusive control of the local factory and office workers. Final decisions on prices, wages, and investment policy, in contrast, must involve the effective influence of the broader community, i.e., the provincial and/or the federal government. Some conflict between the two levels, as was said, is inevitable.

A steadily increasing volume of empirical studies on the subject of industrial democracy does warrant some generalizations which deserve special emphasis. The more effective is the power of the worker: (1) the more likely is his job to be a source of pleasure; (2) the more efficiently does he work; (3) the broader is his range of interests; and (4) the deeper is his sense of community interest, identification, and commitment. In short, the more likely is alienation to be overcome.

In the past few years industrial democracy has become the central common objective of leading trade unionists and socialists in western Europe. From Norway to Italy it has been removed from the dry pages of periodicals and placed on the hot pavement beneath the feet of strikers. Prime Minister Palme of Sweden has acknowledged his country is not yet socialist and sees this new direction as one way of making it so. Chancellor Brandt's Social Democrats were committed to broadening and deepening co-determination in West Germany but insufficient votes necessitated a temporary compromise. And in Italy, auto workers staged a major strike on the issue of local control. The I.L.O. in Geneva has just completed a major study of similar developments and practices in a number of countries.

For the present no one can say with honesty or precision what steps will be taken to implement industrial democracy in Canada. It seems reasonably certain that the changes which come about will be heterogeneous. Most will result initially from extensions of the collective bargaining process. But some will be of the co-determination kind found in West Germany, and some, hopefully, will emerge among the publicly-owned crown corporations of Saskatchewan and Manitoba.

This much having been said, it must also be noted that we shall not likely witness in Canada a major thrust towards industrial democracy in the immediate future. At present a number of people in the English-speaking trade-union movement are committed to it. In the main, however, they are the civil servants within their unions. Trade-union leaders at the national level seem to be either indifferent or hostile to the idea. In Quebec the labour movement at present is embarking in a much more militant and consciously left-wing direction. In the major unions in that province, there now seems to be at leadership and administrative levels an uncommon degree of unanimity concerning the need to move in an open socialist direction. If this is a reflection of the mood and tendencies of French-Canadian workers at the plant level, then the prospects for significant and positive change are very real.

It is clear that an inordinate amount of work and thought will be required. Corporate power, both American and domestic, has deeply conditioned many of us in the wrong direction. Only determined effort to show the need to extend both democratic control at the top and local power in our places of work will enable us to build that civilized society Woodcock so desires. In the foreseeable future we do indeed require more local power. But we also require an expanded state.

In the Dock of History

PATRICK MACFADDEN

The continued exposure to high mountains and low politicians is one of the hazards of life in British Columbia. Radiation from this antic mix produces apoplexy in some, apocalypse in others. George Woodcock may be the latest victim.

We can only judge political actions in a context of opposing forces. Similarly with political systematizing. It cannot take place in a vacuum. The least one should demand from a sociology of politics is that it have some relationship with the real world of men and women. As with politics itself, it must begin, in the old tag, where the masses are.

Where the masses are *not* is in the political terrain occupied by Woodcock. It is safe to say that a social movement advocating the establishment of *phalanstères*, along Fourier lines, in, say, the Kootenays is peculiarly susceptible to the fate traditionally reserved for *a priori* conceptions when exposed to the cold winds of the phenomenal world.

The Conservative call for an "incomes policy" to cure current economic discontents finds its mirror image in the false libertarianism of "stop everything". To demand from mass urban society that it retreat to a rural polity governed by eighteenth-century primitive anarchist theory is to indulge in whimsy, if not cynicism. It may be that we have something to learn, in the abstract, from the Bakuninist strains in the Federation of the Jura of 1880: but politics has to do with the application of principles and not merely with their elaboration. The Woodcock formula means mass pauperization, not just "a reduction in the standard of living for many people".

It is no doubt distressing that ordinary people continue to demand high wages despite Theobald, and good schools despite Illich; that monogamy and child-bearing still top the popularity polls despite the ministrations of Millett and Ehrlich; that Colonel Sanders still has it all over brewer's yeast and spinach, and that Labatt and O'Keefe have survived the massive assaults of Baba Ram Das; and that young people still flock to the cities – cities, as the poet put it, that "wink at them like a wicked uncle" – in order to undergo their age-old and anonymous *rites de passage*; and that citizens still insist on granting assent to the idea of the sovereignty of the people expressed in and through the political state despite the best efforts to save them of Narodnik and English Utopians alike.

Why are Woodcock's formulations so a-historical, even anti-historical? Does he really believe that his verdict on 1789 and 1848 says anything meaningful about the profound implications of the events of those years? Had the Girondins survived, would "fraternity" have survived? To ask the question is to answer it. A leading Girondin, Madame Roland, wrote in the summer of 1791 that a civil war would be "a great school of public virtue. Peace will set us back . . . we can be regenerated through blood alone." So much for the fraternity-loving Girondins whose untimely extinction meant a missed opportunity to be butchers. And so much for selective indignation extrapolated without regard to the motives and results of human action.

Woodcock shrinks from contemplating the daring of the historical act. He throws up his hands in horror. He wishes to go to the country. It is of no consequence to him that the resource-hungry nation-state to the south will cut, like a knife through butter, the life-lines of his utopian, fragmented community of producers. His kibbutzim would last – how long? Perhaps a year. It is said that this should be so. Woodcock's position is well described by Adorno: "Impotent in the machinery of the universally developed commodity relation, which has become the supreme standard, the intellectual reacts to the shock with panic." Woodcock has finally succumbed to panic.

Why should this be so? Because it is easy. The alternative is to face the necessity of choice, for to will a desired end, as he does, must also mean to will the methods necessary to achieve it. The Left tradition, which Woodcock now so vehemently jettisons, always recognized that necessity and that choice. The result is to put the Left in the dock of history, an uncomfortable place compared with being eternally in the well of the court. The verdict as to which is the more honourable position is not yet in. Perhaps it can never be in. And so one has to choose.

An extension of Woodcock's semi-mystical quietism is his inability to elaborate a methodology or a procedure whereby his projections might be effected. Such an elaboration would entail a confrontation, in concrete terms, with the reality of the Canadian state. (In the plea for an anti-nation, Woodcock sometimes seems to slip over into traditional anarchist arguments for an anti-state, which is quite a different matter.)

But it is surely not enough to confess to "an uneasiness amounting to alarm" at the continued presence of nationalism in Canada or anywhere else, not enough to score debating points at the expense of the new African and Asian countries whose nationhood has been won only with great sacrifice and great courage and whose struggle for survival should be an object of sympathy and admiration.

Consider Woodcock's summation: France – a predatory nation, crazy, suffering from an undulating sickness recurring at intervals; the Third World – xenophobic, bureaucratic, led by petty dictators given to blackmail, a danger to humanity, and so on. All this from one who pairs himself with Rosa Luxemburg as being an authentic carrier of the ideal of universal fraternity!

During the period of U.S. expansion in the fifties and sixties,

social scientists were busy writing books on the evils of nationalism. Needless to say, no attempt was made to distinguish among
its various forms: the nationalism of the dominated was held
to be bad, the nationalism of the dominating largely unexamined.
No doubt, removed from time and place, we would all agree
that nationalism is a dubious virtue. However, it is not given
to us to be so elevated. People make their history, as Marx
said, in circumstances not of their own choosing. We are part
of the circumstances. Like the weather, we can only hinder or
help.

It is easier to find agreement with Woodcock's concern over
the growth of the state. The trouble is that he seems to regard
the state as a product of nationalism rather than its forerunner.
In any event, to berate the state simply in terms of its incipient
Leviathanism is to ignore the dialectics that gave rise to Canadian "nationalism" in the first place. The image of the state
supplied by Dreitzel is apposite here: ". . . the boundaries
between state and civil society," he writes, "have been ob-
scured: the state on the one hand acts and functions more and
more as a kind of super-corporation which in various ways is
entangled with private enterprises, while the society on the other
hand has been politicized to an extent where even the remotest
community is not left untouched by the consequences of state
activity."

This picture of the state as a super-corporation, federating,
and mediating among, other giant corporations, is as true of
Canada as it is of the United States, France, and Britain. The
political consequences are striking: to the degree that national
governments need to serve indigenous entrepreneurial interests,
they will from time to time be required to show a proper degree
of hostility towards extra-mural entrepreneurs and towards those
foreign states which act as their spokesmen. Hence, much of
what Woodcock sees as natonalism in Canada is the pained
reaction of native capital finding itself squeezed, in the famous
phrase, "until the pips squeak". Not all of it, of course. There
is a genuine thread of anti-imperialism in the new nationalism.

It is curious that Woodcock reserves his strictures for the nationalism of the Left; business nationalism, it appears, requires no sermons. (And the degree to which the Canadian state is subservient to the interests of its business class may be measured by the decorous alacrity with which Messrs. Benson, Basford, and Mackasey were forced to beat a retreat when recently confronted by the lobbies.)

What Woodcock offers is a flight from the state. This could never be popular. What people encounter in their relations with one another is the state. It is from the state that they have come to expect the fulfilment of their projections. "The state," as Ellul points out, "is expected to provide the answer to every contingency, even in private affairs. The social services are there to settle individual problems." It follows that if the state is no longer able to meet these requirements, it loses legitimacy, and revolution may follow. Something like this appears to be happening in Quebec. Woodcock, of course, would argue that seizure of state power is irrelevant.

Politically, however, Woodcock's alternative, as adumbrated here, makes little impression. It is not entirely clear, for example, what he means by "a socialized community". If he means common ownership of material goods, it is likely that the Canadian army will be on his doorstep; if not, the prospect sounds even drearier than our present anomie. (Mark Kesselman's study of local government in France shows a communal government maintaining consensus by appealing to an apolitical ideology and by exclusion of any genuinely significant local issues. In other words, a bunch of yokels talking about nothing.)

Seen in this light, it is of no consequence to deplore such secondary features as the megalopolis that services the corporations, or to evoke a back-to-the-land ethic that is clearly not in the cards. Any mechanism for moving the human enterprise forward must engage things as they are. This means confronting the state in all of its manifestations instead of indulging in revolutionary defeatism. In British Columbia, for example, it means taking the case for "socialization of the sources of wealth," in Woodcock's phrase, to MacMillan Bloedel, Garfield Weston, Mitsubishi, and Mr. Frank MacMahon, a mission during the completion of which Woodcock may count on the sympathetic and anxious support of all of us. Furthermore, such an outing on his part would go far to satisfy the sceptics among us that the new politics of Aquarianism do not in fact serve as a front office for the old politics of accommodation.

The Epitome of a Colony

D. I. DAVIES

George Woodcock writes as if his vision of Canada is radical and calls for a new social order. Unfortunately, he demonstrates again the conservatism that lies behind his anarchism and the fact that his "plea" is altogether unrelated to the social realities of Canada. The core of his argument is radical enough – that Canadians at all levels be given the opportunity to create for themselves their politics, their economics and their ideologies, something which they have never been able to do until now – but his specific proposals would lead to precisely the opposite condition. Under the Woodcock regime, Canadians would be less independent, less creative and less imaginative than they are at present. Why is this?

Fundamentally, Woodcock's argument is a-historical. Canada is not simply a country with wide spaces, a variety of peoples and infinite resources: it is composed of a set of people who, over the past three hundred years, have been framed by conditions of colonialism and dependency. Since the seventeenth century, Canadians have never been able to define for themselves the kind of society they want. Whether they were Indians, Frenchmen, Irishmen, Scotsmen, or Englishmen, there was always somebody else defining their social "space" for them, and usually his power was located outside Canada's national boundaries. In different ways John Porter in *The Vertical*

Mosaic and Léandre Bergeron in his *Petit Manuel* have emphasized the consequences for internal social relations of this
series of conquests. The "mosaic" of ethnicity, religion, and
class was pyramidal in that power was based on the control of
economic resources, and ethnic and religious hierarchies were
established which corresponded to the various waves of colonial
conquest. The phenomenal variation across Canada in economic
opportunities was caused by the priorities of capitalist development; but the cultures by which people make sense of their
inequalities are now framed by religion, ethnicity, language, and
regional and federal politics, as well as by the "harder" forms
of communication such as technology and physical space.

Canada is, in many respects, the epitome of a colony. Not
only was it created as a colony; the successive "conquests" have
also created a series of colonies within colonies. It is doubtful
whether there is a single country in the world whose *total* consciousness is so permeated at all levels by the experience of
colonialism. Woodcock's interpretation of these experiences is
to ask us to forget the causes of the "mosaic," to admire the
heterogeneity of its effects, and to freeze our politics at *that*
point. In this sense, his analysis is back-to-front. By making the
units of politics these segmented cultures, he allows the dominating capitalism to continue unchecked its divisive and determining course, and by creating false political dichotomies of
city and country he makes it difficult to conceive change as a
series of interactions based on competing power claims, and
thus impossible to see how rural reconstruction, the "regeneration of cities," and a "reversal of the direction of technology"
could be brought about.

But there is a second, and related, objection to Woodcock's
proposals. This lies in his definition of community and the
attempt to create *unanimous* politics at all levels. ("Any decision of any kind that affects only a local group must be
reached by that group alone and by consensus if possible.")
What is totally lacking in Woodcock's politics is the conception
of conflict. The communitarian politics that Woodcock proposes

made in multinational corporation offices in New York. In fact, to set up such bodies which have no power may be counter-effective: the perception of their unimportance may discourage people from involving themselves at all, or else persuade them to turn their attention away from decision-making to preserving the *bonhomie* of the collective. On the other hand, if Woodcock is saying that homogeneous units will generate a demand for self-determination which will create effective decision-making, the existing evidence suggests the contrary. Prince Edward Island, which he cites favourably as being about the right size for a province, is not only in a state of near-bankruptcy but is almost wholly controlled from Ottawa. Small governing communities may result not only in impotence and political indifference but in a further growth of the statism which Woodcock and I would like to avoid. Switzerland, which he picks as his favourite nation, is demonstrably inegalitarian, with three characteristics that are opposed to every element of democracy: it is dominated by a small financial clique, has arguably the most chauvinist attitude to women in Europe, and openly exploits cheap Italian and Spanish labour. What price Apenzell?

The problem is therefore rather to recognize and understand the roots of nationalism than to wish it away by evoking a *Satyagraha* Utopia. And in understanding Canadian nationalism there seem to be three important structural factors: first, that Canada is and always has been a colony; second, that unlike almost all other colonies, a large percentage of its population enjoys a standard of living which is equivalent to that existing in its main metropolitan partner; and third, that there is barely a Canadian national culture which is independent of an alien one (though there is Quebec culture, which is sufficiently removed from France to constitute, as with the Latin American Republics, something close to an indigenous tradition). Somehow the parody of nationalism is a prosperous WASP enclave talking nationalism while carefully checking the *New York Review of Books* and *Ramparts* for levels of sophistication. Our trade unions (outside Quebec) are hardly nationalist, or even conscious (a recent survey shows that international union members are less critical of the United States than all other groups of Canadians). Until evidence is shown to the contrary, we must consider Canadian nationalism (in most of its forms) as another manifestation of middle class *angst* (ranking alongside donations to the United Fund, Oxfam, and visits to the local health-foods store). In terms of its political *threat*, therefore, Trudeau's sense of *real-politik* is probably correct: defuse Hellyer and Gordon by symbolic gestures and keep the pot boiling by inspired Cabinet leaks. After all, Ontario, where most of the wealthy *and* the nationalists live, preferred the status quo in the last provincial election by a deafening bourgeois yawn. Why should it not continue to elect Trudeau?

But of course there is conflict in Canadian society, and there is a definition of politics whch suggests that WASP nationalists have only begun to scratch the surface of conflict. Another Canadian has written that he wants "a democracy for all that will enable the workers and the entire society to make the fullest possible use of the potentialities not only of the economy but of the whole range of human activity and the energies at work in the known universe". The difference, of course, is that Pierre Vallières until recently saw this end as unattainable without violence, because of the corruption and intransigence of the controllers. Whether Vallières was right in seeing violence as *inevitable* is not the point here, but he is surely realistic in seeing that the alternative society can only be born in conflict against the existing system. George Woodcock needs to look around. Canadian history is littered with the bodies of those who dared to attempt to redefine the contours of political and economic relations, and not only in the nineteenth century: the Asbestos strike in Quebec, the loggers strike in Newfoundland, the Winnipeg general strike, the unrest at Simon Fraser University, the *La Presse* strike in Montreal in 1972, Tom Campbell's attacks on the "hippies" in Vancouver, even the troubles at Rochdale College. As I write workers are getting their heads smashed in Nova Scotia, Indians are cramming the penitentiaries (simply because alcohol appears to be the only way left to make their "community" meaningful), and a private strike-breaking force is on the ready in Toronto to fly out at the call of businesses in Hamilton or London whenever the workers want to claim their rights.

These things are happening across Canada, but in only one province has the equivalent of a state of emergency been declared, and only one province has caused the Prime Minister to remark that "there are people . . . who are trying to use the labour movement for political ends, to polarize a class struggle. I think this is very dangerous" (*Globe and Mail*, December 24, 1971). I mentioned earlier that Canada is a colony (and contains colonies within colonies), has no national culture, and includes a large prosperous segment. Quebec (even M. Bourassa) recognizes that it is a colony, but it has the nearest thing to a national culture that Canada possesses and is well aware of the discrepancies between rich and poor. In most respects Quebec contains all the elements of the Canadian mosaic noted by John Porter and George Woodcock (more so than any other Canadian province) and at the same time has an indigenous culture which allows all sections of the population to make sense of their social predicaments in conflictual terms. (Trudeau may deplore it, but he can hardly wish away three hundred years of history.) Because of the heightened consciousness that comes from having a wide range of social differences (class and ethnic) and of possessing a dominant separate culture, Quebec sharpens all the conflicts existing in Canada. In an important sense the *Parti Québecois* speaks for the minorities of Canada – such as the Doukhobors, the Manitoba French, the Indians, the Eskimoes, the Toronto Italians, the Acadians, the Halifax blacks, and the Newfoundland Irish. Corrupted by power, none of the three federal parties speaks for the minorities – and Canada, as Woodcock dimly perceives, is made up of minorities. If we are to look for the new politics, we must start in Quebec.

As the Prime Minister has reminded us only too frequently,

a consciousness of culture is accompanied by a rise in the sense of class struggle. The effect of cultural nationalism or of ethnic consciousness might, at some point, produce a situation in which *different* cultural segments ask the *same* questions about class and power relations. The nationalist groups (as with most middle class radical groups) are therefore providing some of the definitions which will be translated into action by other social classes and ethnic minorities. What they will all have in common (Red Power shows this already) is a resolute opposition to the state and its dominant cultural symbols.

The future is unlikely to be Woodcock's pastoral anarchism. Paraphrasing Marx we may say that Woodcock continues to romanticize about Canada. The point remains to understand and change it.

The Managed Mosaic

DONALD SMILEY

Is Canadian nationalism compatible with pluralism? If we are referring to the mainstream tradition of Canadian *political* nationalism, the answer is clearly "yes". In W. L. Morton's words, Canada was from Confederation "a community of political allegiance alone". But even within the political sphere, this Canadian tradition has provided room for multiple allegiances and identities. From the leaders of the Canada First movement to John Diefenbaker, those Canadians who have emphasized the British connection have been at the same time Canadian nationalists. And in his own structure of political commitments each Canadian has had the opportunity to make his own mix of parochial, provincial, national, and international loyalties. This Canadian nationalism not only permits, but assumes, multiple (though compatible) allegiances.

It is more difficult to be categorical about the relation between the emergent nationalisms of English Canada and Quebec. The credentials of English-Canadian nationalism have nowhere been fully elaborated, although Gar Horowitz has pioneered here. According to Horowitz's formulation, the English-Canadian nation has one crucial dimension of plurality in that, unlike the American, it legitimizes ideological debate on Tory, liberal, and socialist lines. Quebec nationalism appears to an outsider less pluralistic. To a large extent, the English-

Canadian nation – if there be such – and the pan-Canadian nation are creations of the political community; in Francophone Quebec, on the other hand, there is a people, a folk, on whom political institutions of an alien character were imposed. This latter circumstance is perhaps more conducive to a national solidarity frustrating a legitimated pluralism.

The major challenges to the limited state and to Canadian pluralism arise from other sources than Canadian nationalism.

Whatever the dominant characteristic of the Canadian community in the latter part of October 1970, it was assuredly not pluralism. Overwhelming majorities in both Canadian societies cheered on the public authorities as repression was administered. The threats of public order – and the nature of these threats remains in contention – were decisively put down. There was dissent to these policies here and there but none so far as I know from an incumbent of elected executive office in Canada. Power stood with power.

The sovereign of October 1970 was plebiscitary. The claims of political leaders to take action against actual and apprehended terrorism – and to displace the usual processes of public decision in so doing – were based on the legitimacy of the power of those who had been successful in prior elections. Plebiscitary democracy may be defined as a regime in which those who exercise final and authoritative power are exclusively sustained by and restrained by the wills of individual citizens, without the mediation of either private groups or of political institutions less immediately responsive to citizen opinion. It is not perhaps coincidental that immediately before the October crisis federal Liberal leaders were talking in extravagant terms of "guaranteeing" and "enshrining" and "entrenching" individual rights through a constitutional charter. The shift from the formulations of Thomas Paine to those of Thomas Hobbes was made, quite literally, overnight on October 16. Under the new circumstances of crisis, the major problem becomes not that of limiting the powers of government but rather that of determining how governments might protect individuals from one another. Thus the Prime Minister in defending his actions warned that the next target of terrorism might be "you, or me, or some child". Similarly, his Minister of Justice elaborated a new absolutism: "Indeed if there are any absolute rights they reside in the right, both moral and legal, of the democratically constituted authorities to protect the rights and liberties of citizens." The atomistic nature of human society, however, remains in both formulations of human rights, and Pierre Trudeau, like Hobbes, made a smooth transition from absolute individualism to absolute authoritarianism.

The inherently coercive nature of the power of the state was revealed in all its starkness during the October crisis. But our sovereign shows a more benign face in less critical times. In a brilliant article on the operative philosophy of the Trudeau administration Bruce Doern says, "much of it seems to be congruent, on a philosophical plane, with those political scientists who have argued we ought to view the political system in cybernetic terms as a goal-seeking and error-correcting information system that will 'learn how to learn' ". The evidences of the new directions are everywhere: the influence of those with a systems-management orientation in the Trudeau entourage; the elaboration of the emergent orthodoxy in the Report of the Task Force on Information and in some of the publications of the Department of Communications; the renewed emphasis on highly rationalized procedures for policy-making in the Cabinet and the federal bureaucracy; the centralization of information functions in Information Canada; the beginnings of government-sponsored survey research on popular attitudes; federal sponsorship of the new public policy research institute under Ronald Ritchie.

If Doern is accurate, the new Ottawa orthodoxy is of crucial importance to human freedom in Canada. There is enough evidence in the literature of political science and sociology to convince me at least that the disposition of those who think and act as if society were a cybernetic system is to believe in the high priority of systems-maintenance, in the "dysfunctionality" of the institutions and processes which do not contribute to stability, consensus, legitimacy, and incremental adjustment. Here is the challenge to a genuine Canadian pluralism in which there exist centres of power independent of the central authorities.

In the new formulation Canada is indeed to be a mosaic, but a managed mosaic. The Task Force on Information spoke of a category of citizens called "the unreached" outside the communication system of Canadian life; Information Canada is busily remedying this deficiency and has assumed a role in moral uplift with its horrendous posters elaborating such banal admonitions as "Canadians: Stand Together, Understand Together" and "Learn, Baby, Learn". It has been the thing to do for Ottawa to convene conferences of the poor. There is federal organization and financial help for activating such deprived groups as the Indians, and residents of the inner city. Government officials organize tenants' unions in public housing. Policies towards official language minorities, and now towards other cultural groups, inevitably have the effect of making formerly private associations, at least in part, agents of the public authorities. The Department of the Secretary of State emerges as the paymaster of the counter-culture of youth. New developments are no doubt in the offing. Scandal has it that consideration is being given in Ottawa to plans for limited collective-bargaining rights to members of the armed forces and involuntary guests of federal penitentiaries. Scott Young, in an issue of the *Globe and Mail*, suggests a way in which the interests of security and those of protest may be made compatible by government erected "Boo Bunkers" in which home-grown and foreign dignitaries might be exposed to demonstrators without the leaders coming to physical harm.

The new developments in the swallowing of the social by the political are a continuation of trends that have been with us for decades. "Amateur" sport became the recipient of federal largesse in the early 1960's. Most significant artistic, scientific, and cultural activity is within the realm of public support. The private university tradition is almost gone, and many intelligent Catholics have come to believe that the separate school systems in the provinces have come to resemble the public school so much as to be incapable of imparting a genuinely religious education. Private welfare agencies are increasingly being relegated to a subordinate and supplementary role.

We have now in Canada a combination of circumstances dangerous to the values of a limited and pluralistic community: the plebiscitarian dispositions of the political culture, our characteristic deference to authority, our characteristic of preferring the claims of the political when this conflicts with other forms of power; the increasing rationalization of the processes of public decision-making; the ongoing extension of the public authorities into matters formerly social. The senior reaches of Ottawa are firmly in the grip of Karl Mannheim's "bureaucratic conservatism" in which the thrust is to "hide all problems of politics under the cover of administrations"; the new processes of public choice involve the ranking and weighting of objectives in a way inherently hostile to the claims of autonomous centres of social power. Can anyone seriously believe that effective challenges to the social, economic, and political order can be made by groups relying on federal organizational and financial support? Could an ethnic association which had become heavily dependent on public funds survive severe ethnic tensions involving the community? So far as the counter-culture is concerned, the federal leash on Rochdale College and the C.Y.C. has already been shortened. Elsewhere, the Amish and the Hutterites in maintaining *their* counter-cultures show a great deal more sophistication about the realities of state power than do such beneficiaries of federal support as Rochdale, the Toronto Homophile Society, and the publishers of *Guerilla*. Even under benign circumstances, private associations dependent on the state are corrupted as their tests of their own performance and that of their leadership comes largely to be success in deriving financial support from government. I judge this latter is now the case with university presidents.

We badly need a rethinking of the limits of the legitimate power of the state. I have no confidence that our Canadian tradition and the ways in which we are travelling give us much help. We are concerned with individual privacy, and strident expressions of "possessive individualism" call for a lifting of the restrictions on our freedom to bemuse ourselves with alcohol or drugs and for abortions on demand. But such privatization is no barrier to tyranny, and a rational tyrant would work towards assuring that his subjects were so satisfied with the purely private aspects of their lives that they would be dissuaded from autonomous social and political activity challenging his power. Our Canadian tradition fails us in another direction. The story has often been told of how Canada has developed through a symbiotic relationship between government and private economic enterprise. A similar relation has come into existence between the political and the social, and it seems that the operative rule of most Canadians has become that if some worthy purpose is to be accomplished outside the purely private sphere of individual life, the public authorities are legitimately to be involved. The euphemism is "partnership" but in such a relation, government, almost by its natuure, is dominant.

I will here sketch out three fragmentary suggestions for a programme of pluralist reform:

First, there is an urgent need to redress the balance between the plebiscitary and non-plebiscitary elements of the political system in favour of the latter. In particular, the domestication of the House of Commons should be stopped. When the House is true to its traditions it cannot be made to fit into any cybernetic design. It is, or should be, not part of a feedback loop in a communications system but an arena of political conflict in which those who govern are required without the visible accoutrements of high office to confront, each sitting day, those whose business it is to discredit and ultimately to displace them. Neither is the House in any genuine sense a legislative body. It began a very long time ago, and should so remain, an assembly convened by the executive to find out what exactions those influential in the local communities of the land would tolerate. The Trudeau regime has had some success in diverting members from this representative and essentially obstructionist role by extending the activities of committees and letting M.P.'s delude themselves that they are American-type legislators. The Opposition has been too willing to accept the doctrine that their role is to be "constructive". It may well be that through public acceptance of the Liberal doctrine of the absolute right of the governors to govern, as embodied in the current Rules, Canadians can be made to forget – if they ever knew – that in some critical circumstances resistance to government is the ultimate safeguard of freedom. In the recent changes in procedures, Canada has given up, to its great peril, the possibility of parliamentary obstruction.

Second, we must destroy the monolithic nature of provincial systems of public education. Nowhere was John Stuart Mill more prescient than when he wrote in 1859 in "On Liberty"

> If government would make up its mind to require for every child a good education, it might save for itself the trouble of providing one. . . . A general State education is a mere contrivance for moulding people to be exactly like one another and as the mould in which it casts them is that which pleases the predominant power in the community, whether this be a monarch, a priesthood, an aristocracy, or the majority of the existing generation; in proportion as it is efficient and successful, it establishes a despotism over the mind, leading by natural tendency to one over the body.

In no area of activity are the requirements of bureaucratization and rationalization less compelling than in education, and in no part of our Canadian life have those been pressed with so little resistance. Frank MacKinnon's wise and imaginative book of a decade ago, *The Politics of Education,* puts forward one plan for reform which deserves serious, if belated, consideration. Education must be high on the pluralist agenda.

Third, we need to protect the sphere of private, family economic enterprise. I am delighted that the socialists of Saskatchewan have come to a recognition of the claims of the family farm — or, more accurately, of the farm family. This sphere of genuine private enterprise has nothing to do with General Motors or the Aluminum Company of Canada and is not to be defended in terms of the old shibboleths of capitalism like consumer sovereignty or the rational allocation of resources through a system of competitive prices. The entrepreneurial ethic, and a way of individual and family life based on that ethic, should be preserved for those who want it in the name of pluralism and as an alternative to the bureaucratic milieu in which most of us live and work.

A programme of reform along the directions I have suggested should logically await a philosophical defence of the credentials of the limited state and the pluralistic Canadian community. As my colleague Jack McLeod has perceptively pointed out, most of the limited disposition of Canadians to philosophize about politics has been directed towards the themes of federalism and nationalism, and little systematic attention has been given to liberal democracy. We have had, for example, nothing like the Hart-Devlin debate in England on the relation of law and morality or the continuing discussion of the competing claims of freedom, order, and equality in the decisions of the Supreme Court of the United States. Where is there a serious discussion of equality in the reports of recent federal commissions on bilingualism and biculturalism, women, Indians, and youth? Apart from Denis Smith's recent book, how is it that the October crisis did not spark a serious debate on freedom and order in Canada? Why is it almost impossible to come by a philosophic treatment of human rights in the voluminous literature arguing for and against the entrenchment of such rights? How is it that such an official report as that of Ronald Ritchie on the establishment of an institute for public policy research should be allowed to make so many questionable assumptions (assumptions about, for example, the relation of knowledge to power and to social change, and about the capacity of social science for prediction) and yet go unchallenged except by James Eayrs? In my mind this task of fundamental re-examination of our values is made more urgent because there is in Ottawa an emergent orthodoxy, a way of thinking and acting with broad but unexamined consequences for human dignity in Canada.

Will a rethinking of our fundamental political values take place within Canadian universities? Our newest Nobel prize-winner has made the case for the freedom of scientific research in a way not duplicated by any Canadian humanist or social scientist. In terms of challenges to our autonomy there are nihilist and anti-intellectual pressures from some elements in our universities who judge us by our commitments rather than our capacities for analysis. But there are other young people who are going no further than to ask insistently, and I think justifiably, that at least some of us some of the time turn our attention to first-order questions of political and social life. What in my judgment is infinitely more dangerous than these pressures are those from the public authorities for short-run, applied, and purportedly scientific research, research of the kind suggested by Mr. Ritchie, "aimed not at making or proposing policies but adding to the information and tools of analysis of those who do make them and of the public who accept and are subject to them". With such bureaucratic pressures for scholars to justify themselves, what are the pay-offs of the work of an Innis, a Creighton, a McPherson, a George Grant? Or of the Pierre Elliott Trudeau of a decade ago?

My own tentative and amateurish attempt to work out the credentials of the limited state and the pluralistic community goes like this. Government is inherently and irremediably coercive. The state thus cannot make people good or happy or creative, but should properly be limited to removing obstacles to their own efforts to become so. It legitimately ensures the maintenance of physical life; it is acting illegitimately when it attempts to provide its citizens with reasons for living. It can properly in most circumstances demand compliance with its decrees, but it can command respect only when such is freely given. It must be kept out, not only of certain individual areas of life, but also of crucial spheres of social activity.

But the limited state is inevitably the pluralistic community. Power cannot be restricted by anything so fragile as constitutional charters but only by autonomous centres of countervailing power. Pluralism need make no extravagant claims. Its credentials are not those of participatory democracy by which public decisions are legitimated only by involving all affected persons in making them. Nor is there any reason for pluralists to accept the pieties that there is an invisible hand guiding the community towards justice if only power is sufficiently fragmented, or that truth will inevitably emerge from the marketplace of clashing ideas and ideals. The claims of pluralist democracy, and they are crucial, are that only this kind of regime has resources to avoid the tyranny of its rulers impressing unimpeded their own limited sympathies and interests on the political community.

The Anti-politics of the Anti-nation

FRANK CASSIDY

What does it mean to create a nation? Woodcock would have us believe that a nation is a single centralized, authoritarian state. He urges us to give up the advocacy of nationalism and to look instead to federalism – the participatory principle – as the answer to the woes of Canada. He argues that we must discard the revolutionary tradition of the left and the example of Marx and Engels in order to create an anti-nation in the spirit of Jean Jacques Rousseau's federalism. Yet it was Rousseau who advanced the spirit of patriotism as a substitute for the commercialization of the spirit in the market society. It was Rousseau who urged the Polish to create a strong "national character" if they wished to create a true federalism. And it was Rousseau who defended the nation, the pattern of habits and customs, as the foundation of the public space which would give people the opportunity to be citizens in the real and forgotten sense of the word.*

*For Rousseau's writing on nationalism, see *Considerations on the Government of Poland* (1772) and *Constitutional Project for Corsica* (1765), which are translated and reprinted in *Rousseau's Political Writings*, Frederick Watkins, ed. (Toronto: Nelson, 1953). Rousseau also discussed nationalism in *A Discourse on Political Economy* (1755) and in the "Dedication" to *A Discourse on the Origins of Inequality* (1755). Both of these works are translated in *The Social Contract and Discourses*, G. D. H. Cole, ed. and trans. (New York: E. P. Dutton, 1950).

Canadian nationalism is not a disease, an infectious paranoia. Rather, the facts of the Canadian situation require a new National Policy. In the process of overcoming the power of the United States to use its advanced technology to establish a multinational economy, the Canadian nation will be recreated. This nation will be the first step towards a new internationalism, an internationalism not based upon the exploitation of Canadian resources, but upon the equality of nations and peoples who have achieved that self-determination which must be the basis of responsible, meaningful citizenship. The actual political activity of all those Canadians who, at present, are unable to control their own experience, must establish a new political space within Canada. But before uniting, in order to unite, the Canadian people must re-establish the nation, the set of habits, shared experiences, and interest, as the foundation of this political space.

Although he is best known as the author of *The Social Contract*, Rousseau was one of the first political theorists to see the importance of nationalism in modern times. He advocated nationalism because he hoped it would be a way to create or conserve an active political life, to decentralize political responsibility. He did not see politics as the struggle over the uses of the coercive power of a centralized state. Instead, he saw that politics must be redefined from an active point of view, that politics is an activity by which the masses of people solve the problems of their social and economic life. Like Woodcock, Rousseau advocated a "rigorous devolution of power", maintaining that federalism is meaningless unless citizens, united by common ties, control their own experience. It was in this context that he evaluated the uses of the nation.

In order to counter a situation in which "men are forced to caress and destroy one another at the same time . . . [and] are born enemies by duty and knaves by interest", Rousseau sought to create a new politics, an active politics, which was based on the solution to the question of inequality. In 1772 he advised the Poles "to move the hearts of men and to make them love their fatherland and its laws . . . through institutions which seem idle and frivolous to the superficial man, but which form cherished habits and invincible attachments". Seeking to revive the spirit of public purpose and service, he advocated a nationalism which was not a myth fashioned to obscure the realities of social inequality, but "a fine and lively feeling" which would support and unite people in their struggle against inequality. He did not urge the Poles to create a nation because it would give them a strong bureaucratized state. Rather, he hoped the nation would supplant the state as we know it, and be the foundation of a state of a new type: a state that did not stand above its citizens, a state that was the outgrowth of their own political activity.

The position of Poland in the eighteenth and nineteenth centuries was similar in many ways to the position of Canada today. Its independence was constantly endangered by the aspirations of the greatest power of reaction in its time, the Czarist autocracy of Russia. A divided, weakened Poland was crucial to Russia's hopes of expansion because of its central location, just as a "friendly", available Canada is crucial to the interest of American corporate capitalism because of its supply of resources and its ready consumer market. Rousseau hoped nationalism would place Poland in a position to resist her enemies. "The virtue of citizens," he wrote, "their patriotic zeal, the particular way in which national institutions may be able to form their soul, this is the only rampart which will always stand ready to defend her, and which no army will ever be able to breach."

Yet we should note that Rousseau did not advocate nationalism and "patriotic zeal" in all situations. In particular, he did not support the blind obedience and the mindless chauvinism which we have come to know as patriotism. Maintaining that an essential aspect of political life is that the interest of the citizen and government be one and the same, he argued that men could not be expected to respect their country "if their lives, liberty, and property lay at the mercy of persons in power, without their being permitted or its being possible for them to get relief from the laws. For in that case . . . the word 'country' would mean for them something merely odious and ridiculous."

As with so many of his ideas, Rousseau's nationalism has become a forgotten ideal because of his failure to understand the realities of modern life. In a world soon to be dominated by the ethic of capitalism, he sought to return to the democratic city-state of antiquity. In a society soon to be destroyed by the drive of industrialization, he urged the Poles and Corsicans to devote themselves to agriculture and the simple tastes of rural life. Despairing over the inhumanities of the market economy, he counselled a withdrawal from the modern world and a return to the past. Much like Woodcock, he placed his trust in "a simpler existence where work would be done for joy rather than money". Much like Woodcock, he proposed a radical de-centralization of power, a confederation of many small states to a country that was about to be overwhelmed by a strongly centralized power.

Among Rousseau's many mistakes, and this may also be said of Woodcock, perhaps there was none so central as his failure to place the national question within the social and political context of his times. His distaste for centralization of any sort and for the requirements of modern economics, were positions which, if followed, would weaken any chances of achieving the very goals he sought. But his ideal of the nation lives on as a testament to a nationalism which is not the "militaristic, bureaucratic, xenophobic" sort of the great imperialist powers today.

It is impossible to talk about the national question without admitting that there may be different types of nationalisms. There is the nationalism of the oppressor and oppressed, the exploiter and exploited, the dominator and dominated, of those who use technology to control people's experience and those whose experience is controlled. It is inadvisable to evaluate the meaning of Canadian nationalism until these distinctions are made.

Nationalism, internationalism, and federalism are not eternal essences which exist above the tides of history. Rather, they are specific strategies which peoples use to forward their interests within specific social and economic situations. Depending upon this situation, nationalism can be of the chauvinistic kind that Woodcock writes of, or it can be an application of the principle of internationalism. The concept of nationalism as the advocacy of a single, centralized, and authoritarian state rests upon the reification of one historical manifestation of nationalism, the nationalism of the traditionally dominant states of Europe. Ignoring distinctions between different types of nationalism, Woodcock withdraws into his own internal world of meaning. He proposes the "control by a community of producers over their means of work" while ignoring the fundamental impediment to this control: the real power which the United States exerts over the lives of the Canadian people. There is no recognition of the obstacles in the way of internationalism: the sacred ideal of *internationalism*, the word itself, takes the place of everything.

Woodcock considers the growth of the Canadian nationalist movement to be similar to the recurrent support that the revolutionaries of the nineteenth century gave to national movements. So then, perhaps it would be useful to take a look at the basis of this support. For example, Marx and Engels' advocacy of the nationalism of countries which were the colonies of larger powers was based on their analysis of the best political strategy to bring about a true internationalism based upon equality rather than domination. They maintained that "the worker has no fatherland", for they knew that he was faced with the power of an expanding capitalist accumulation that knew no national boundaries. But this did not lead them to reject nationalism. Rather, it led them to look into the dominant realities of this situation and to scrutinize and advocate those emerging realities which were providing the basis for the reorganization of class society along the lines of a true international community.

Consequently, Marx and Engels based their support for the

national movements in Poland and Ireland on the principle that "an international movement of the proletariat is possible only among independent nations". They held the view that the Irish and Poles "are internationalists of the best kind if they are very nationalistic", for as Engels wrote, "No great people can seriously discuss its internal problems as long as national independence is absent."

Woodcock would have it otherwise. He would have one nation practise true internationalism in a world of nations; one state disappear before the eyes of its citizens in a world of states; one people control its experience in a world which is out of its control. He would dispel the shadow of the castle and conjure an image of a simple, tranquil, and innocent Canada free from the anxieties of the super-powers. But this wish is for naught. For the state and the nation are still bound within the walls of the castle.

We live on the threshold of a "post-nationalist age", but it is not the age of the anti-nation. It is the age of the new mercantilist internationalism of the great corporations. The super-powers are blasting down the walls of the weaker nations and securing their resources and markets. We do not need a weakening of Canadian governmental institutions; we need the growth of those institutions which will provide the barriers within which a nation of politically active citizens can reassert their power to determine the future of Canada. This is the only remedy for the political disintegration that is accompanying the rapid growth of American influence in Canada.

Canadian nationalism is rooted in the question of control. The construction of strong national barriers to the encroachments of corporate capitalism is the only insurance that Canadians will not be absorbed within an economy they do not control. Ironically, the disastrous possibilities of this situation bring to mind the economic absorption and subsequent cultural disintegration of the Ihalmiut of the Central Barrens as described by Farley Mowat in *People of the Deer*. Perhaps a lesson in the dangers of depending on an economy which is controlled elsewhere can be learned from Canada's destruction of its own North.

Long before the North became a valued base of resources, the People of the Deer roamed the Central Barrens trapping the "Tuktu" in the manner of their fathers. But in the 1920's the women of Toronto, New York, and London, the fashionable women of the salons, wanted the fur of the fox to cover their shoulders in the chill of the evening. Spurred by profit, white men went to the Barrens and convinced the Ihalmiut to give up their bows and arrows and to use rifles to hunt fox. The People became good hunters and they received food in return for their fox pelts. But one day the white men left; the fine women of the cities no longer desired the fur of the fox. Soon there were no shells for the rifles. The People had forgotten the ancient ways and many died. "By the middle of the fifties," Farley Mowat sadly reported, "the Ihalmiut were in effect a dead race."

If Canadians are not to suffer a similar fate, the economic institutions of the federal government must be strengthened. There must be a centralization of economic power and a decentralization of the control over this power. Canadians must unite by creating a new national policy. But this will not be the national policy of the Bank of Montreal or of the Conservative party. It will be the national policy of the workers in the factories, the farmers on the Prairies, the students in the schools, and of all those in Canada who, at present, are subject to the needs of another economy.

National liberation is a precondition for the growth of responsibility among the citizens of Canada. The nation must be the basis on which a true federalism will be built. This federalism will arise out of the struggle of the Canadian people to free themselves from the chains of exploitation both domestic and foreign. This federalism will have no relationship to the federalism of Switzerland – that ancient "experiment" in true participatory democracy in which women were allowed to vote for the first time in federal elections in 1971. Canadian federalism will be based upon a resolution of the social inequalities that make political liberty, at present, an impossibility.

The Beginning of
the Long Dash

SAM AJZENSTAT

The necessary conditions of a distinctive, national self-expression threaten, in being achieved, to alter that self-expression beyond recognition and undermine its distinctiveness. To live as Canadians may mean the death of what it has been to be Canadian. As George Woodcock points out, economic and cultural self-determination, without which our federal system is unlikely to survive, is itself a threat to that system's vitality. This is only one of a group of similar dilemmas that currently converge in the problem of Canada and in whose dialectic Woodcock is caught.

Woodcock starts with an easy distinction between good and bad nationalisms. "The great task of Canadians in the 1970's is to shake themselves free" of that "complex and insidious American colonialism" under which we fell in escaping the simpler British variety. We are to do this in order to preserve what he calls "the independent, pluralistic, and unpredictable way of life which Canada offers to the courageous". The bad nationalists, the "ranting xenophobes and cold-minded centralizers" press beyond this modest goal to demand our exclusive loyalties to a nation-state.

For Woodcock, as for most of us, the importance of economic independence lies largely in what we could or would do once we had it. Woodcock, as it turns out, makes it the basis of a total transformation of our economic and political life. This obliges him to show that the uses of our independence, as he sees them, will not entail the more virulent brand of nationalism. As he pursues this project one can begin to sympathize with the logic of the xenophobes and centralizers, even while regretting the enthusiasm with which they embrace the inevitable.

It is instructive that Woodcock does not explain how we are to free ourselves of U.S. imperialism without centralizing, just as he does not go into the question of who exactly are the "many people" who will somehow have to be prevailed upon to accept the by-now proverbial "reduction in the standard of living", that dubious progenitor of moral and spiritual values. How, short of centralized planning, are we to distribute evenly the economic burdens and rewards of independence?

Woodcock's answer is that the responsibility for distribution and its co-ordination would lie with participatory, decentralized local associations and larger groupings into which they and others would "coalesce". Far from opposing nationalism to decentralization, Woodcock counts on an extreme decentralization to keep nationalism pure. In Woodcock's argument the problem – whether Canada can achieve viable self-determination without coercive power (the issue of nationalism) – comes to depend on whether small regions within it can be so designed as to have viable self-determination without coercive power (the issue of decentralization). This in turn poses the question whether an individual can achieve self-determination without coercion (the issue of participation). One problem winds down through three levels (four if we count the issue of internationalism), and on each Woodcock's answer has to be that self-determination does not entail coercion.

Crucial to Woodcock's argument is the issue of participation. In it lies both the motive and the defence for his theory of decentralization. It also carries the fundamental flaw in the structure. Woodcock rests his faith in the imminence of a post-national world where politics "shall have to" be conducted by "co-operation, consensus, and participation" carried on "in those places where men meet face to face" and replacing "coercion and confrontation". This presumably will ensure the concurrent realization of whatever of liberty, equality, and fraternity is available to us. Hence, he adds that "above all characteristics the society of the future must be based on voluntary decisions".

But when we are told that the requirement of voluntary decisions is compatible with the requirement that confrontation be avoided and consensus sought, we ought to suspect a hidden premise. What shall we do with those whose voluntary decisions consistently bring them into conflict and confrontation with others? Shall they be sent, with a note reading "does not participate well with the other children", to a psychiatric social worker who will register a diagnosis of false consciousness and prescribe tranquillizers and a visit to the socialization centre?

The hidden premise, obviously enough, is that conflicts of interest are sufficiently unnatural or artificial to allow us to hope for a political system based on common interest. Granted that Woodcock admits "it is impossible to conceive that all conflicts of interest will be eliminated" in the post-national world, but he clearly wishes it were possible and he does believe that "the socialization of the sources of wealth would be likely to reduce them".

Woodcock evades not only the question of how coercive we might have to be to eliminate conflict and confrontation, but also the question of whether the conflict he appears to hate might not be fundamentally bound up with the qualities of independence, unpredictability and courage which he appears to cherish – for some a superficial linkage that "socialization of the sources of wealth" could break easily; for others a matter of elementary psychological processes.

Our best learning theories link learning with acquisitiveness. On the other hand, some free schools hold an ideal of learning which places a high value both on community and on the infant's "natural curiosity". These schools have hardly faced the dilemma that curiosity is acquisitiveness, the bent of whose liberty is not towards the communal values of equality and fraternity but rather towards hierarchical élites based on evaluation of skill and fierce and divisive competition.

While much more is required both of argument and counter-argument, I would venture the tentative conclusion that there is no individualism but possessive individualism. An individual or a group achieves self-definition and self-determination only through self-assertion, interfering with its own members and with others. Politics occurs in the attempt of my self-determination to cope with that of others by accommodation or conflict.

We still know very little about the mechanics of such coping. There is, for example, much to learn from theories like R. D. Laing's about what people are really doing to one another when they "reach a consensus" or "participate in decision-making". The lesson appears to be that human relations consist of an ineradicable conflict between individuality (or liberty) and community (or equality-fraternity) which plays into the hands of hierarchy.

There is also, of course, an extremely narrow rim containing those moments of unified individuality and community that make us call a relationship "love", even when for the most part it too is politics. The narrow rim is a part of what we call private life and the private-public distinction is the only viable way we have of hedging part of our lives against hierarchy, leaving a place open for those happy accidents like a good marriage, where individuality and community can coexist.

But we cannot design a politics on the expectation of happy accidents. There are certainly such things as common interests, perhaps even at times a general will or a collective apprehension of truth. It would, however, be irresponsible to insist on the point in our politics and make consensus the only means to peace, order, and good government. Consensus is not so important to us that we should ensure it by means of an educational system designed to make our children forget the distinction between community and its public counterfeit.

Individuality too has its public counterfeit; so we must not, like some liberals, make pure individuality any more than pure community the touchstone of our political life. The public counterfeits of individuality and community are alienation and hierarchy. They are what individuality and community must turn into when they enter the wider arena where they, like the men whose drives they are, have to be in conflict with each other. At the same time, though counterfeits are "copies", they are not purely negative. They are, for the most part, the way we come out of ourselves towards others, and they generate that process of growth which is possible only through conflict. We cannot live without them but we cannot live either without places of secret calm where we replenish our strength before returning to the cave we call politics.

However, it is precisely the bent of participatory democracy, ideals of consensus and face-to-face encounter proposed by Woodcock and his strange bedfellows of the counter-culture, to destroy the distinction between the public and the private. When that distinction is lost, it is never politics that is destroyed. Hierarchy reasserts itself while subtler things are lost.

This is why it is neither paradoxical nor even surprising that the revolutionary tradition "in preaching the universality of man . . . has encouraged nationalism and in preaching international liberation has promoted imperialism". Universalism and libertarianism must be missionary faiths that verify themselves by making all men co-extensive with the nation of the faithful.

This could also explain why democratic socialism can survive only on the belief that the socialization of the sources of wealth will not substantially reduce conflicts of interest but may very well accentuate them. For, if there must be hierarchy, we ought to prefer the hierarchy of alienation that does not pretend to be community or individuality to the one that does; for from the latter there is no escape. What worries me are indications that democratic socialism, faced with an influx into the political system of people who have been taught to hate hierarchy and alienation, is finding itself forced into the pretense of being able to eliminate both.

To tell people that radical decentralization, workers' control, referendum, initiative, or recall can substantially alter the possibilities of political life is only to compound the enormous frustration that centuries of disastrously false political theory have wrought.

The surest part of my argument is that decentralized politics is at least as hierarchical as any other. But I am inclined to claim – though with much less certainty or clarity – that it would turn out to be much more so. In part it is my image of small towns, close-knit neighbourhoods, and encounter groups as the true seats of stifling socialization and entrenched élites that makes it seem plausible to me that the smaller a group is, the more it will tend to claim the total life of its members.

On the other hand, I can value these tendencies as a counterweight to the alienation of more remote and anonymous groupings as much as I value that alienation as a counterweight to them. That at least is the theory. But it is extremely difficult to say what the interaction between local and remote élites really does to the power of each, or how it operates. To get at some of these issues I want to propose – with some trepidation – a rather cynical scenario of Woodcock's decentralized ideal:

Woodcock proposes that constituencies be made smaller and more homogeneous and given more power with respect to broader groupings. Within the smallest groups the result would in fact be to strengthen the hand of the local power structures, informal decision-making cliques dependent on socialization and machine-style politicking. At the same time, these local powers – able to recall only their own representatives – would find it largely impossible to control the broader constituencies. The referendum would be a useless instrument of control, for with each small grouping representing only one apparently cohesive set of interests, the higher levels would find it comparatively easy to play the local groups off against each other on the principle of divide and rule. One great strength of the provinces at present is that their governments come to the federal level representing something like an aggregated coalition of diverse interests, so that what the municipalities of Ontario may lose with respect to rural Ontario they can make up with respect to the municipalities of other provinces.

A claim put forward on behalf of an entire province is likely to be broad and forceful enough to be difficult for a federal government to get around. At the same time it is generalized and ambiguous enough (except in Quebec) to be fairly easily aggregated, at least to an extent, into a comprehensive federal programme. The demands of homogeneous, radically decentralized localities, on the other hand, will be both weak enough so that larger groups can easily ignore them and sufficiently clear-cut and uncompromising that they will all but have to ignore them.

Any referendum is likely to display a combination of individual caprice, local interest, regional rivalry, and diversity of political philosophy, which, in the absence of middle-level agencies for aggregating opinion, will tend to preclude any clear-cut mandate. Upper levels will find themselves in possession of practically unlimited power, and that not merely in the affairs within their jurisdiction. We know already that where comparatively larger groupings control distribution of goods, they will not find it difficult to regulate production as well.

The emphasis on consensus at the lowest level will rob dissenters of the respectable power base of an official opposition. Worse still, the individual will find himself stuck in dozens of interlocking hierarchies, trying to absorb what his representatives are willing to tell him of the results of the proliferating series of public and private meetings between producers and producers, consumers and consumers, producers and consumers, farm and city, city and city, farmers in one region with farmers in another, each with the entire region, and region with region – all passionately trying to form viable blocs, while higher levels of government, if they are smart, will schedule two referendums a day until the people cry out for respite and open beer parlours on voting days.

So, local governments, at the same time as they find themselves more powerful in their localities, are frustrated in the attempt to use their power base against broader groupings, while the power that comes more and more to reside in the central government must be exercised in the context of a diminished sense of national unity and consequently of increasing resentment. This state might well, by virtue of its power to plan, be "socialist". It would only dubiously be democratic.

Only two alternatives would be open to such a policy: to reinstate something very like the provinces as middle-range aggregating devices able to balance federal power without fragmentation while providing a formal structure for viable opposition, or an increasing appeal to charismatic leadership.

Thus Woodcock is right to praise Canadian federalism – though for the wrong reason. It does not represent a half-hearted half-step to libertarianism but is rather a generally effective and, fortunately, rather responsive system of stable, hierarchical government.

Anything we try to do with our economic independence may well upset the delicate balance of our present dominion-provincial relations. However, the logic of self-defeat is not as obvious to me here as in the case of decentralization. So my tentative conclusion is that if we are to have our nationalism and still retain whatever we have of an irregular, pluralistic (and so on) way of life, we must *not* decentralize radically. Whatever national mission we end up with must be hammered out in the clash of provincial hierarchies. This will set limits on the possibilities of economic planning that the Left may find galling. Then there is always the chance that the momentum of world-wide social change may overwhelm the fruitful divisiveness of our federalism. But when the choice is between the risk of nationhood and the *reductio* of radical decentralization, we are justified in taking the risk.

This conclusion may appear to mitigate the claim that we cannot have the good nationalism without the bad. This is partly because that claim is a matter of a rather abstract analysis. The enormous list of other factors with which nationalism would have to interact in the concrete makes the risk very difficult to evaluate and the chance worth taking, unlike the decentralization option whose delusiveness lies in the promise rather than in the problems of implementation.

But the "optimism" of my conclusion is also partly due to the circumstance that only one aspect of nationalism is being discussed here. In a broader context that I cannot now enter into – the cultural, educational, and social – our choice, I cannot help believing, is between our own crass philistinism and someone else's. I suppose, wistfully, that our own is preferable. But that is the issue of a broader and much more complicated discussion.

A Note on the Contributors

VIV NELLES is an Assistant Professor of History at York University, Toronto. He is now completing a book on the politics of resource development in Ontario.

ABRAHAM ROTSTEIN is an Associate Professor of Economics at the University of Toronto. He is managing editor of *The Canadian Forum* and has written numerous articles on foreign investment in Canada, and on Canadian nationalism.

GEORGE WOODCOCK is the founding editor of *Canadian Literature* and a free-lance writer. His previous publications include some forty volumes, the most recent being *Gandhi, Dawn and the Darkest Hour: A Study of Aldous Huxley, Canada and the Canadians, Into Tibet,* and, in collaboration with Ivan Avakumovic, *The Doukhobors. Herbert Read: The Stream and the Source* and *The Rejection of Politics and Other Essays* are being published in late 1972.

DESMOND MORTON is Associate Professor of History at Erindale College, University of Toronto. He is the author of *Ministers and Generals* and *The Last War Drum.*

CHRISTIAN BAY teaches political science at the University of Toronto. The author of *The Structure of Freedom*, he has also contributed articles to *The Canadian Journal of Political Science* and *Our Generation.*

NORMAN WARD is Britnell Professor of Political Science in the Department of Economics and Political Science at the University of Saskatchewan. He has written, or contributed to, several books on Canadian government and politics, among them

Democratic Government in Canada, and has contributed to such periodicals as *The Canadian Journal of Political Science* and *The Canadian Forum.*

GEORGE RAWLYK teaches history at Queen's University, Kingston. He has edited several volumes of articles and documents dealing with the Atlantic provinces and is the author of *Yankees at Louisbourg.*

BRUCE HODGINS is Associate Professor of History at Trent University, Peterborough. He is the author of several articles on Confederation, and in 1971 published a biography of John Sandfield Macdonald.

EDWARD BROADBENT is the member of Parliament for Oshawa-Whitby and author of *The Liberal Rip-off.*

PATRICK MACFADDEN teaches journalism at Carleton University, Ottawa. He is one of the editors of *Last Post.*

D. I. DAVIES is a teacher of sociology at York University, Toronto. He is the author of several books, including *Social Mobility and Political Change,* and was co-editor of *Social Space.* A further book, *The Management of Knowledge,* is in preparation.

DONALD SMILEY is Professor of Political Science at Erindale College, University of Toronto and author of the *Canadian Political Nationality.*

FRANK CASSIDY teaches political and social theory at Simon Fraser University in Burnaby, B.C.

SAM AJZENSTAT is an Assistant Professor of Philosophy at McMaster University in Hamilton.